Anonymous

The Application of the Benzidine Colours in all Branches of

Printing

Anonymous

The Application of the Benzidine Colours in all Branches of Printing

ISBN/EAN: 9783337306823

Printed in Europe, USA, Canada, Australia, Japan

Cover: Foto ©Thomas Meinert / pixelio.de

More available books at **www.hansebooks.com**

THE

APPLICATION OF THE BENZIDINE COLOURS

IN

ALL BRANCHES OF PRINTING.

FARBENFABRIKEN

VORM.

FRIEDR. BAYER & CO., ELBERFELD.

Published by the

FARBENFABRIKEN vorm. FRIEDR. BAYER & CO., ELBERFELD.

1899.

Sole Representatives for Great Britain and Ireland:

The Elberfeld Farben Fabriken Company Limited

MANCHESTER, 20, Booth Street, Mosley Street.
BRADFORD, 18, Vicar Lane.
GLASGOW 42, Bothwell Street.
LONDON, 19, St. Dunstan's Hill E. C.

No. 677. 1899.

Preface.

Fifteen years have now elapsed since the Benzidine colours made their appearance in the market, and at that time no one imagined the important part they would play in improving many branches of textile manufacture. Although at first their application was almost exclusively used in dyeing, it soon became apparent that they would make great headway for all requirements in printing.

The Benzidine colours are suitable for padding, they can also be discharged white and coloured, and with their assistance mercerised effects can be produced etc. They are used in many different ways for printing cotton, wool and silk goods, and indeed without their aid, modern printers would feel a great void.

In the accompanying pamphlet we present you merely with an illustrated collection of the chief applications of our important Benzidine dye-stuffs, trusting it may always keep before you the advantages, the utility and the various applications of these colours.

Farbenfabriken vorm. **Friedr. Bayer & Co.**

Elberfeld, Summer 1898.

Cotton printing.

.

Padding.

The following Benzidine colours are suitable for padding:

Red Dyestuffs:

Benzo Purpurine 1 B, 4 B
Brilliant Geranine B, 3 B
Geranine G.

Orange Dyestuffs:

Benzo Orange R
Chloramine Orange G
Congo Orange G
Mikado Orange.

Yellow Dyestuffs:

Brilliant Yellow
Chloramine Yellow
Chrysamine G, R
Chrysophenine
Direct Yellow R
Mikado Yellow
Yellow P R
Thiazole Yellow.

Green Dyestuffs:

Benzo Dark Green
Benzo Green G, B B
Benzo Olive.

Blue Dyestuffs:

Benzo Blue 2 B, 3 B
Benzo Chrome Black Blue B
Benzo Cyanine B, 3 B, R
Benzo Sky Blue
Benzo Sky Blue 4 B
Benzo Black Blue G, 5 G
Brilliant Azurine B, 5 G
Brilliant Benzo Blue 6 B
Brilliant Sulphon Azurine R
Diazo Blue Black
Diazo Black B (undiazotised).

Violet Dyestuffs:

Benzo Violet R
Heliotrope B B.

Brown Dyestuffs:

Benzo Brown B X, G, N B X, 5 R, B R,
    R extra
Benzo Chrome Brown B, G, R, 3 R, 5 G
Benzo Dark Brown
Chloramine Brown G
Congo Corinth G
Diazo Brown R extra
Direct Bronze Brown
Direct Fast Brown B, G G
Hessian Brown B, B B, M M
Toluylene Brown B, B B O, M, R.

Grey Dyestuffs:

Benzo Fast Black
Benzo Fast Grey
Benzo Grey S extra
Pluto Black B, G, R.

Table 1.

The Benzidine colours are used to a great extent in **padding** or **finishing** light shades on Aniline Black patterns or for covering colour prints.

They are padded in the usual manner on the slop padding or finishing machine, whether they be padded with watery solution of Benzidine colour or slightly thickened with dextrine or mucilage of tragacanth or whether the solution of Benzidine dyestuffs be added to the particular quantity used for finishing.

No. 1.
1 oz. or 48 grms. **Benzo Brown B X**
2 „ „ 100 „ phosphate of soda
12½ galls. „ 100 litres water.

No. 2.
1 oz. or 50 grms. **Benzo Violet R**
2 „ „ 100 „ phosphate of soda
12½ galls. „ 100 litres water.

No. 3.
3½ oz. or 65 grms. **Geranine G**
5 „ „ 100 „ phosphate of soda
31½ galls. „ 100 litres water.

No. 4.
½ oz. or 25 grms. **Benzo Chrome**
Black Blue B
2 „ „ 100 „ phosphate of soda
12½ galls. „ 100 litres water.

No. 5.
3½ oz. or 70 grms. **Benzo Chrome**
Brown G
5 „ „ 100 „ phosphate of soda
31½ galls. „ 100 litres water.

No. 6.
4½ oz. or 303 grms. **Thiazole Yellow**
2½ „ „ 187 „ **Brilliant Benzo**
Blue 6 B
1½ „ „ 100 „ phosphate of soda
10 galls. „ 100 litres water.

No. 7.
1 oz. or 50 grms. **Benzo Black Blue 5G**
2 „ „ 100 „ phosphate of soda
12½ galls. „ 100 litres water.

No. 8.
3½ oz. or 65 grms. **Chloramine Yellow**
5 „ „ 100 „ phosphate of soda
31½ galls. „ 100 litres water.

No. 9.
½ oz. or 24 grms. **Brilliant Benzo Blue 6 B**
2 „ „ 100 „ phosphate of soda
12½ galls. „ 100 litres water.

TAB. 1.

Cotton printing.
(Colours for paddings.)

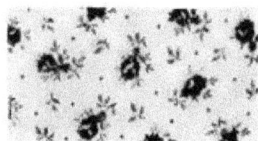

1

**Benzo Brown BX padded on
Aniline Black.**

2

**Benzo Violet B padded on
Aniline Black.**

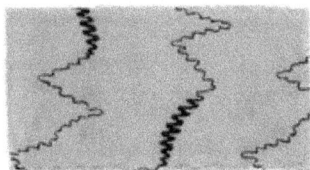

3

**Geranine G padded on
Aniline Black.**

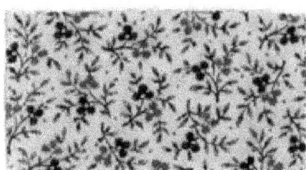

4

**Benzo Chrome Black Blue B padded
on Aliz. Red and Aniline Black.**

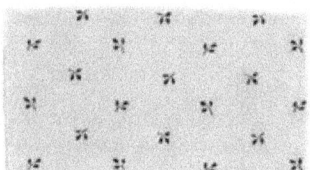

5

**Benzo Chrome Brown G padded on
Aniline Black.**

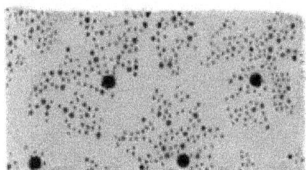

6

**Brilliant Benzo Blue 6B and Thiazole
Yellow padded on Aniline Black.**

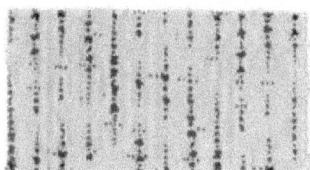

7

**Benzo Black Blue 5 G. padded on
Alizarine Red S N extra.**

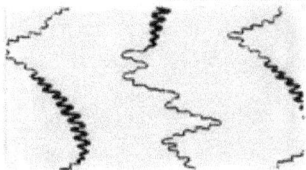

**Chloramine Yellow padded on
Aniline Black.**

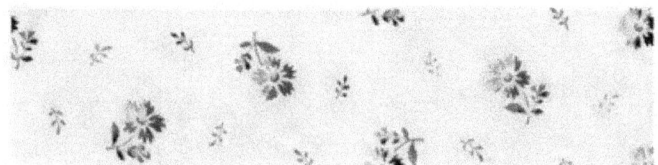

9

Brilliant Benzo Blue 6B padded on colour prints.

FARBENFABRIKEN vorm. FRIEDR. BAYER & Co. ELBERFELD.

7

No. 10.

½ oz. or 24 grms. **Chloramine Orange G**
2 „ „ 100 „ phosphate of soda
12½ galls. or 100 litres water.

No. 11.

1 oz. or 50 grms. **Benzo Green G**
4 „ „ 200 „ phosphate of soda
12½ galls. or 100 litres water.

No. 12.

10 oz. or 500 grms. **Bril. Benzo Blue 6 B**
2 „ „ 100 „ phosphate of soda
12½ galls. or 100 litres water.

No. 13.

½ oz. or 25 grms. Chrysamine G in powd.
2 „ „ 100 „ phosphate of soda
12½ galls. or 100 litres water.

No. 14.

½ oz. or 37,5 grms. **Benzo Fast Black**
1½ „ „ 100 „ phosphate of soda
10 galls. „ 100 litres water.

No. 15.

3 oz. or 100 grms. **Benzo Violet R**
1 „ „ 60 „ **Benzo Sky Blue**
3 „ „ 200 „ phosphate of soda
10 galls. or 100 litres water.

No. 16.

4 oz. or 200 grms. **Benzo Sky Blue**
4 „ „ 200 „ phosphate of soda
12½ galls. or 100 litres water.

No. 17.

10 oz. or 500 grms. **Geranine G**
2 „ „ 100 „ phosphate of soda
12½ galls. or 100 litres water.

No. 18.

5 oz. or 250 grms. **Chloramine Yellow**
2 „ „ 100 „ phosphate of soda
12½ galls. or 100 litres water.

No. 19.

½ oz. or 24 grms. **Benzo Cyanine B**
2 „ „ 100 „ phosphate of soda
12½ galls. or 100 litres water.

Tab. 2

Cotton printing.

(Colours for paddings.)

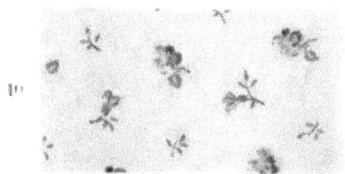

10 Chloramine Orange G padded on
colour prints.

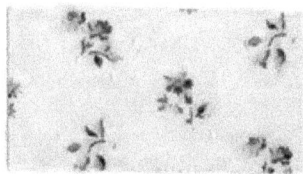

11 Benzo Green G padded on
colour prints.

12 Aniline Black padded with
Brilliant Benzo Blue 6 B.

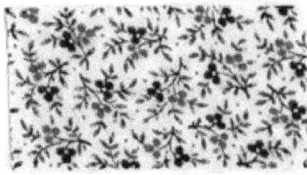

13 Chrysamine G padded on Alizarine Red
and Aniline Black.

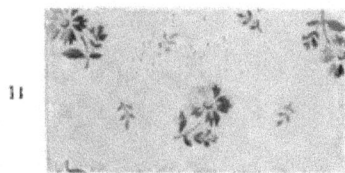

14 Benzo Fast black padded on
colour prints.

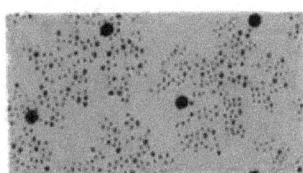

15 Benzo Violet R and Benzo Sky Blue
padded on Aniline Black.

16 Aniline Black padded with
Benzo Sky Blue.

17 Aniline Black padded with
Geranine G.

18 Aniline Black padded with
Chloramine Yellow.

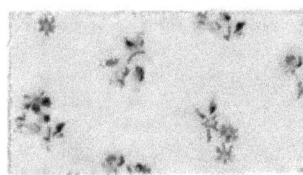

19 Benzo Cyanine B padded on
colour prints.

FARBENFABRIKEN vorm. FRIEDR. BAYER & Co., ELBERFELD.

The Benzidine dyestuffs are also used for slop padding goods printed with the modern ice-colours.

No. 20.

Ice Red (Paranitraniline)
β-Naphtol

8 oz. or 400 grms. Benzo Sky Blue
2 „ „ 100 „ phosphate of soda
12¼ galls. or 100 litres water.

No. 22.

Ice Blue (Dianisidine)
β-Naphtol

8 oz. or 400 grms. Geranine G
2 „ „ 100 „ phosphate of soda
12¼ galls. or 100 litres water.

No. 24.

Ice Bordeaux (α-Naphtylamine)
β-Naphtol

8 oz. or 400 grms. Chloramine Yellow
2 „ „ 100 „ phosphate of soda
12¼ galls. or 100 litres water.

No. 26.

Ice Black (Benzidine)
Developer E S

5 oz. or 250 grms. Bril. Benzo Blue 6 B
2 „ „ 100 „ phosphate of soda
12¼ galls. or 100 litres water.

No. 21.

Ice Blue (Dianisidine)
β-Naphtol

5 oz. or 250 grms. Chloramine Yellow
2 „ „ 100 „ phosphate of soda
12¼ galls. or 100 litres water.

No. 23.

Ice Bordeaux (α-Naphtylamine)
β-Naphtol

8 oz. or 400 grms. Benzo Sky Blue
2 „ „ 100 „ phosphate of soda
12¼ galls. or 100 litres water.

No. 25.

Ice Red (Paranitraniline)
β-Naphtol

12 oz. or 600 grms. Brilliant Geranine B
2 „ „ 100 „ phosphate of soda
12¼ galls. or 100 litres water.

No. 27.

Ice Bordeaux (α-Naphtylamine)
β-Naphtol

4 oz. or 200 grms. Benzo Green G
1 „ „ 50 „ Chrysophenine
2 „ „ 100 „ phosphate of soda
12¼ galls. or 100 litres water.

No. 28.

Many Benzidine Colours such as Benzo Nitrol Brown G, Benzo Nitrol Dark Brown N, Direct Fast Brown B, Direct Blue Black B, Pluto Black B etc. possess the property of combining with diazotised Paranitraniline and producing effective styles fast to washing.

Should the resulting product differ in shade from the original dye very fine two-coloured effects can be obtained, such as are produced with Toluylene Orange G (Pattern 28). After diazotised Paranitraniline has been printed on, steam for 5 mins., and then soap, wash and dry.

Cotton printing.
(Slop-padded shades on Ice colours).

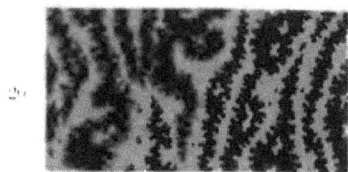

Ice Red padded with Benzo Sky Blue.

Ice Blue padded with Chloramine Yellow.

Ice Blue padded with Geranine G.

Ice Bordeaux padded with Benzo Sky Blue.

Ice Bordeaux padded with Chloramine Yellow.

Ice Red padded with Brilliant Geranine B.

Ice Black padded with Brilliant Benzo Blue G B.

Ice Bordeaux padded with Benzo Green G and Chrysophenine.

Dyed with G Toluylene Orange G, printed with diazotised Paranitraniline.

FARBENFABRIKEN vorm. FRIEDR. BAYER & Co. ELBERFELD

Direct Printing.

The following Benzidine Colours can be printed on cotton material:

Red Dyestuffs:

Benzo Purpurine 1 B, 4 B, 6 B
Brilliant Congo G
Brilliant Geranine B, 3 B
Congo Red 4 R
Congo Rubine
Delta-Purpurine 5 B
*) Geranine G
Rose Azurine B, G.

Orange Dyestuffs:

Benzo Orange R
Congo Orange G
Mikado Orange 3 R, 4 R
Toluylene Orange G.

Yellow Dyestuffs:

Chloramine Yellow
Chrysamine G, R
Chrysophenine.

Green Dyestuffs:

Benzo Green G
Benzo Olive.

Blue Dyestuffs:

Azo Blue
Benzo Azurine G, R
Benzo Blue RW, 3 B
Benzo Cyanine 3 B
Benzo Sky Blue
Benzo Black Blue G, 5 G
Benzo Chrome Black Blue B
Brilliant Benzo Blue 6 B.

Violet Dyestuffs:

Azo Violet R
Benzo Violet R.

Brown Dyestuffs:

Benzo Brown B, G G, N B
Benzo Chrome Brown R, B, G
Congo Corinth G
Chloramine Brown G
Toluylene Brown B, M, R.

Grey Dyestuffs:

Benzo Fast Black
Benzo Grey S extra
Direct Blue Black B
Direct Deep Black T.

Black Dyestuffs:

Direct Blue Black B
Direct Deep Black T.

---

*) becomes somewhat faster when acetate of chrome is used.

Table 4

The Benzidine Colours have become generally adopted in direct cotton printing especially for such articles where no great importance is attached to fastness to washing.

By adding albumen water for print colours, greater fastness to washing is obtained and many Benzidine colours become faster to washing if acetate of chrome be used.

No. 1.
Grey.

1 pint   or 200 grms. **Print Colour A**
3 pints „ 600   „   mucilage of tragacanth
                     65 : 1000
1 pint   „ 200   „   water.
           1000 grms.

Print Colour A.
Boil :

2 oz. or   20 grms. **Direct Blue Black B**
8 oz. „   80   „   wheat starch and
4½ pints „ 880 „   water, and then add
2 oz. „   20   „   phosphate of soda.
           1000 grms.

No. 2.
Pink.

½ pint   or 150 grms. **Print Colour B**
4½ pints „ 850   „   mucilage of traga-
                     canth 65 : 1000
           1000 grms.

Print Colour B.
Boil :

4 oz. or   40 grms. **Brilliant Geranine B**
8 oz. „   80   „   wheat starch
4½ pints „ 880 „   water, and then add
2 oz. „   20   „   phosphate of soda.
           1000 grms.

No. 3.
Violet.

The same as above in No. 1
       but instead of Direct Blue Black B
       Benzo Violet R.

No. 4.
Blue.

The same as above in No. 1
       but instead of Brilliant Geranine B
       Brilliant Benzo Blue 6 B.

No. 5.
Blue.

¼ pint   or 50 grms. **Print Colour C**
3 pints „ 600   „   mucilage of traga-
                     canth 65 : 1000
1½ pints „ 350   „   water.
           1000 grms.

Print Colour C.
Boil :

2 oz. or   20 grms. **Benzo Sky Blue**
8 oz. „   80   „   wheat starch and
4½ pints „ 880 „   water, and the add
2 oz. „   20   „   phosphate of soda
           1000 grms.

No. 6.
Yellow.

Boil :

1 oz. or   10 grms. **Chloramine Yellow**
3½ pints „ 635   „   water
5 oz. „   50   „   wheat starch
1½ pints „ 300   „   mucilage of traga-
                     canth 65 : 1000,
                     and then add
½ oz. „   5   „   phosphate of soda
           1000 grms.

13

No. 7.

Orange.

1½ pints or 500 grms. **Print Colour D**
8½ pints „ 500 „ mucilage of tragacanth 65 : 1000

1000 grms.

Print Colour D.

Boil:

2 oz. or	20 grms	**Congo** Orange G	
8 oz. „	80 „	wheat starch and	
4½ pints „	800 „	water, and then add	
2 oz.	20 „	phosphate of soda	

1000 grms.

No. 9.

Blue.

(Colours for padding).

1½ pints or 125 grms. **Print Colour E**
3 pints „ 300 „ mucilage of tragacanth 65 : 1000
5½ pints „ 575 „ water.

1000 grms.

Print Colour E.

Boil:

4 oz. or	40 grms.	**Benzo Blue 3 B**	
8 oz. „	80 „	wheat starch and	
4½ pints „	860 „	water, and then add	
2 oz.	20 „	phosphate of soda	

1000 grms.

Brown.

(Print Colour).

Boil:

4 oz. or	40 grms.	**Benzo Brown N B**	
8 oz. „	80 „	wheat starch and	
8½ pints „	700 „	water, and when	
		cold add	
2½ pints „	120 „	albumen water 1 : 1	

1000 grms.

No. 8.

Olive.

(Print Colour).

Boil:

4 oz. or	40 grms.	**Benzo Green G**	
7 oz. „	70 „	wheat starch	
3½ pints „	775 „	water, and then	
½ pint „	100 „	mucilage traga-	
		canth 65 : 1000	
2 oz. „	20 „	phosphate of soda	

1000 grms.

(Colours for padding).

1½ pints or 125 grms. Olive (Print Colour)
8½ pints „ 425 „ mucilage of tragacanth 65 : 1000
2½ pints „ 250 „ water.

1000 grms.

No. 10.

Brown.

Boil:

2½ oz. or	25 grms.	**Benzo Chrome**	
		Brown G	
8 oz. „	80 „	wheat starch and	
4½ pints „	575 „	water, and then add	
2 oz. „	20 „	phosphate of soda	
		and finally when	
		cold add	
2 pints or	400 „	albumen water	
		1 : 1 250	
1 pint „	200 „	mucilage of traga-	
		canth 65 : 1000	

1000 grms.

After printing and drying, steam without pressure for ½ — ¾ — 1 hour according to requirement. The goods are then either finished direct, or slightly soaped, washed and dried.

Table 1

Cotton printing.

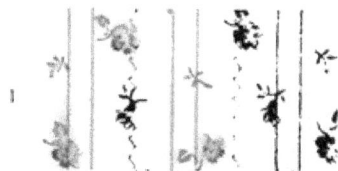

Cover Print: Direct Blue Black B
over coloured print.

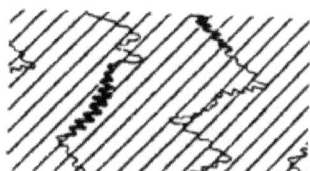

Cover Print: Brilliant Geranine B
over Aniline Black.

Cover Print: Benzo Violet R
over coloured print.

Cover Print: Brilliant Benzo Blue 6 B
over coloured print.

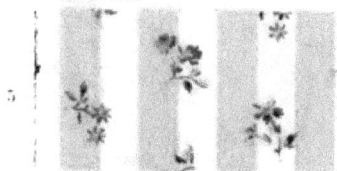

Cover Print: Benzo Sky Blue
over coloured print.

First Print: Aniline Black.
Cover Print: Chloramine Yellow.

Cover Print: Congo Orange G
over coloured print.

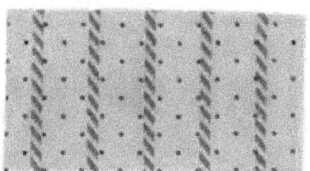

Benzo Green G padded and printed.
Cover Print: Fast Black.

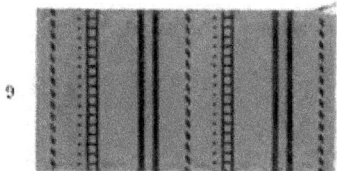

Padded: Benzo Blue 3 B.
Printed: Benzo Brown N B.

Benzo Chrome Brown G.

FARBENFABRIKEN vorm. FRIEDR. BAYER & Co., ELBERFELD.

Padding.

Table 2.

To imitate certain woven cloths the cotton material is padded on the machine, on one side, then dried and covered with Fast Black, and then steamed ¾ hour without pressure and finished.

No. 1.

Dissolve:

¾ oz.	{	10 grms.	**Congo Orange G** in
5 pints	{	1500 „	water.
		Boil	
2½ pints	{	2500 „	mucilage of traga- canth 65:1000
1½ lbs.		800 „	wheat starch and
3½ pints	{	2887 „	water.

10000 grms.

No. 2.

¾ oz. or 10 grms. Chrysophenine
other proportions same as given in No. 1.

No. 3.

Dissolve:

¾ oz.		15 grms.	**Benzo Chrome Black Blue B** in
6½ pints	{	1000 „	water.
		Boil	
2½ pints	{	2500 „	mucilage of traga- canth 65:1000
1 lb.		800 „	wheat starch and
2½ pints	{	2887 „	water.

10000 grms.

No. 4.

¾ oz. or 10 grms. Geranine G
other proportions same as given in No. 1.

No. 5.

Dissolve:

1½ oz.	{	12.5 grms.	**Benzo Green G** and
½ oz.		5.0 „	Chrysophenine in
2½ galls.	{	3592.5 „	water.
		Boil:	
11½ pints	{	2000 „	mucilage of traga- canth 65:1000
4 lbs. 6 oz.		700 „	wheat starch and
15 pints	{	2000 „	water.

10000 grms.

No. 6.

¾ oz. or 10 grms. **Benzo Fast Black**
other proportions same as given in No. 1.

No. 7.

¾ oz. or 10 grms. **Brilliant Geranine B**
other proportions same as given in No. 1.

No. 8.

¾ oz. or 10 grms. **Brilliant** Benzo Blue 6B
other proportions same as given in No. 1.

No. 9.

¾ oz. or 10 grms. **Benzo** Violet R
other proportions same as given in No. 1.

No. 10.

¾ oz. or 10 grms. Benzo Chrome Brown R
other proportions same as given in No. 1.

Fast Black.

3 pints or	300 grms.	**Fast Black**	
6½ pints „	620 „	acetic acid starch tragacanth thickening	
2½ noggins	80 „	acetate of chrome 32° Tw.	

1000 grms.

Cotton Printing
(padded).

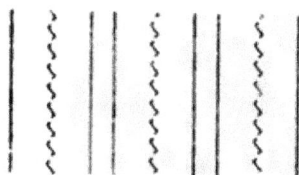

| 1 | | 2 |

Congo Orange G.   **Chrysophenine.**

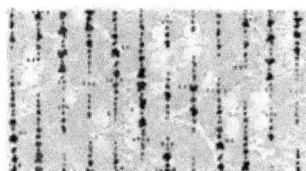 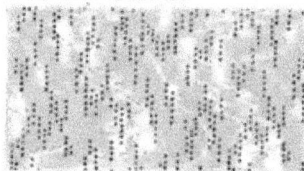

| 3 | | 4 |

Benzo Chrome Black Blue B.   **Geranine G.**

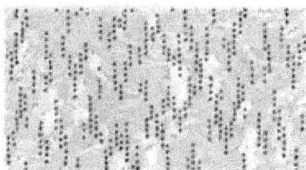 

| 5 | | 6 |

Benzo Green G and Chrysophenine.   **Benzo Fast Black.**

 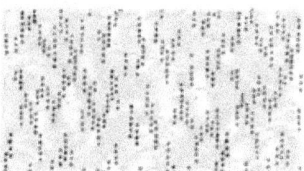

| 7 | | 8 |

Brilliant Geranine B.   **Brilliant Benzo Blue 6 B.**

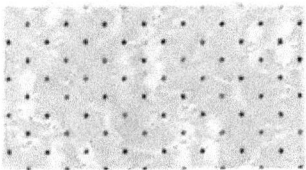 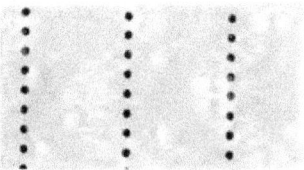

| 9 | | 10 |

Benzo Violet R.   **Benzo Chrome Brown B.**

FARBENFABRIKEN vorm. FRIEDR. BAYER & Co., ELBERFELD.

Dyeing after printing.

Cotton goods are frequently printed with Aniline Black and afterwards dyed at the boil with Benzidine Dyestuffs. This is done in an alkaline bath, or for light delicate shades in a bath containing common salt. Most of the Benzidine colours are suitable for this process.

Dyed with:

No. 1.
3 % **Benzo Blue R W.**

No. 2.
3 % Benzo Blue R W; after dyeing treat with sulphate of copper for ½ hour at the boil, thereby being rendered much faster to light.

No. 3.
3 % **Congo Orange G.**

No. 4.
3 % **Brilliant Geranine B.**
10 % common salt.

No. 5.
1 % **Heliotrope B B**
  1 % soda
  1 % Turkey red oil. Dye at 176° Faht. lift, and add 20 % Glauber's salt, then boil for ¼ hour.

No. 6.
3 % Chrysamine G.

No. 7.
3 % **Benzo Purpurine 10 B.**

No. 8.
3 % **Benzo** Nitrol Brown G; after washing and drying, run through a mangle with diazotised **paranitraniline.**

No. 9.
1 % **Benzo Chrome Black Blue B.**

No. 10.
1 % Chrysophenine
1 % **Brilliant Benzo Blue 6 B**
10 % common salt.

1

Aniline Black;
dyed with 3% Benzo Blue R.W.

2

Aniline Black; dyed with
3% Benzo Blue R.W. and coppered.

3

Aniline Black;
dyed with 3% Congo Orange G.

4

Aniline Black;
dyed with 3% Brilliant Geranine B.

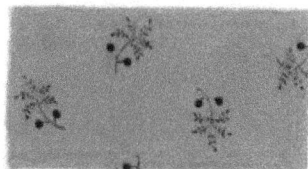

5

Aniline Black;
dyed with 1% Heliotrope B.B.

6

Aniline Black;
dyed with 1% Chrysamine G.

7

Aniline Black;
dyed with 3% Benzo Purpurine 10 B.

8

Aniline Black; dyed with
3% Benzo Nitrol Brown G and afterwards
treated with Paranitraniline.

9

Aniline Black; dyed with
4% Benzo Chrome Black Blue B.

10

Aniline Black; dyed with
1% Chrysophenine
and 1% Brilliant Benzo Blue 6 B.

FARBENFABRIKEN vorm. FRIEDR. BAYER & Co., ELBERFELD.

No. 11.
Dyed with **Benzo Purpurine** 4 B;
cover printed with **Aniline** Black.

No. 12.
Dyed with Benzo Sky Blue;
cover printed with Aniline Black.

No. 13.
Dyed with 4°° **Benzo Azurine G** in an
alkaline bath;
cover printed with **Aniline Black.**

No. 14.
Dyed with 3°° Benzo **Purpurine 4 B** in an
alkaline bath;
cover printed with Aniline **Black.**

No. 15.
Dyed with **Benzo Purpurine** 4 B;
cover printed with **Aniline Black.**

No. 16.
Dyed with Azo Violet;
cover printed with Aniline Black.

After oxidizing, run through a weak solution of silicate of soda, wash and dry.

Printing of Basic Dyestuffs (without tannic acid) on dyed Benzidine ground.

The basic dyestuffs can not only be dyed on Benzidine colours without a mordant, but they can be printed on without any addition of tannic acid to the colour thickenings, and when afterwards steamed are tolerably fast to washing.

No. 1.
Dyed with:

3°° **Chrysophenine.**

Cover printed with:

Dissolve:

1 oz. or	10 grms.	**Brilliant Green** in
1½ pints „	290 „	water, then thicken with
3½ pints „	700 „	acetic acid starch tragacanth thickening
	1000 grms.	

No. 2.
Dyed with:

2°° Brilliant **Benzo Blue 6 B.**

Cover printed with:

Dissolve:

½ oz. or	5 grms.	Diamond Fuchsine in
1½ pints „	295 „	water, then thicken with
3½ pints „	700 „	acetic acid starch tragacanth thickening
	1000 grms.	

No. 3.
Dyed with:

3°° **Congo Orange G.**

Cover printed with:

Dissolve:

½ oz. or	5 grms.	**Methyl Violet** 2 B in
1½ pints „	295 „	water, then thicken with
3½ pints „	700 „	acetic acid starch tragacanth thickening
	1000 grms.	

No. 4.
Dyed with:

1°° **Geranine G.**

Cover printed with:

Dissolve:

½ oz. or	10 grms.	Methylene Blue BB in
1½ pints „	290 „	water, then thicken with
3½ pints „	700 „	acetic acid starch tragacanth thickening
	1000 grms.	

Steam for ½ hour without pressure, soap cold for 2 minutes and then wash and dry.

Cotton printing
(dyed before printing)

Tab. 7

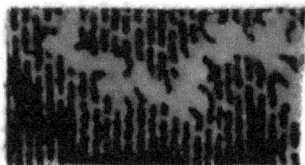

11

**Dyed with: Benzo Purpurine 4 B.
Cover printed with: Aniline Black.**

12

**Dyed with: Benzo Sky Blue.
Cover printed with: Aniline Black.**

13

**Aniline Black
printed on 4°/₀ Benzo Azurine G.**

14

**Aniline Black
printed on 3°/₀ Benzo Purpurine 4 B.**

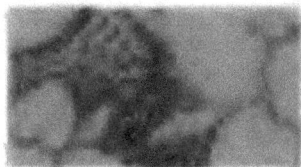

15

**Aniline Black
printed on Benzo Purpurine 4 B.**

16

**Aniline Black
printed on Azo Violet.**

Printing of basic colours (without tannin)

1

**Dyed with: 3°/₀ Chrysophenine,
Cover printed with 1°/₀ Brilliant Green.**

2

**Dyed with: 2°/₀ Brilliant Benzo Blue 6 B.
Cover printed with:
4°/₀ Diamond Fuchsine.**

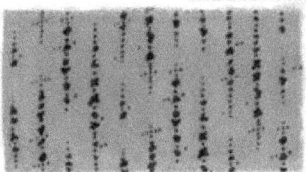

3

**Dyed with: 3°/₀ Congo Orange R. Cover
printed with: 4°/₀ Methyl Violet 2 B.**

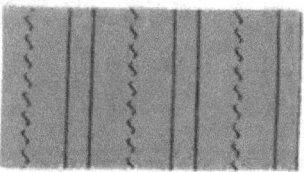

4

**Dyed with: 4°/₀ Geranine G. Cover
printed with: 1°/₀ Methylene Blue B G.**

FARBENFABRIKEN vorm. FRIEDR. BAYER & Co. ELBERFELD

Table 5

Bronze Printing.

Cotton piece goods dyed with **Benzidine** dyestuffs are often printed with Bronze colours.

This can be done in various ways. The bronze colours can be thickened with albumen water, then printed and steamed, or first print on with varnish, and then strew bronze over the material, then allow to dry and brush.

The bronze colours are fixed only on those parts which were printed with varnish.

A third way is by printing on certain varnishes and bronze colours together.

$7\frac{1}{2}$–$8\frac{3}{4}$ lbs. or 300–350 grms. Bronze colour (I.. Auerbach & Co., Furth i Bavaria)
$1\frac{1}{4}$ gallons „   500   „   egg albumen water] l
$\frac{1}{2}$ gallon–3 pints 300–400 „ mucilage of tragacanth (G. Jess.

1300 grms.

Nos. 1, 3, 5, 6, 9, 10, = $7\frac{1}{2}$ lbs. or 300 grms. Rockgold Flux fine
Nos. 2 and 8, = $8\frac{1}{2}$ lbs. „ 350 „ Patent Moss Green
Nos. 4 and 7, = $7\frac{1}{2}$ lbs. „ 300 „ Aluminium Ia.

Print, with brush furnishers, on damped goods, then dry and steam for 10–15 minutes without pressure.

The cotton goods are dyed at the boil with Benzidine colours for 1 hour with the addition of:

per 10 gallons water   per litre water
$\frac{1}{4}$ lb. 1 lb.   or   25 g–100 grms. Glauber's salt.
2 oz.–4 oz.   „   1–2   „   soda ash.

The following were dyed with:

No. 1. 2% **Brilliant Benzo Blue** 6 B.   No. 2. 8% **Pluto Black B.**
No. 3. $3\frac{1}{2}$% **Benzo Green G.**   No. 4. 4% **Benzo Purpurine 10 B.**
No. 5. 4% **Benzo Violet R.**   No. 6. $1\frac{1}{2}$% **Benzo Chrome Brown B**
                                              $1\frac{1}{2}$% **Benzo Chrome Brown R.**
No. 7. 6% **Benzo Chrome Black Blue B.**   No. 8. $1\frac{1}{2}$% Benzo Fast **Black.**
No. 9. 4% **Benzo Purpurine** 4 B.   No. 10. 4% Benzo Blue **B X.**

The following recipe can be recommended for preparing a solution of India-rubber for printing.

Dissolve 2 parts of India-rubber waste (mixed and dried together) with:
4   „   camphor oil
4   „   naphtha, then mix with
1   „   good varnish.

Cotton printing.

(Bronze prints).

Dyed with: 2 Brilliant Benzo Blue 6 B.

Dyed with: 8 Pluto Black B.

Dyed with: 3 Benzo Green G.

Dyed with: 1 Benzo Purpurine 10 B.

Dyed with: 4 Benzo Violet B.

Dyed with: 11 Benzo Chrome Brown B
12 Benzo Chrome Brown R

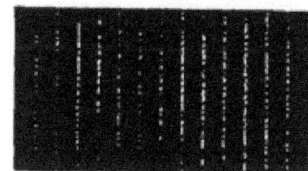

Dyed with:
6 Benzo Chrome Black Blue B.

Dyed with: 4 Benzo Fast Black.

Dyed with: 4 Benzo Purpurine 4 B.

Dyed with: 4 Benzo Blue BX

FARBENFABRIKEN vorm. FRIEDR. BAYER & Co., ELBERFELD.

When dyed on cotton the following Benzidine colours can be discharged with acetate of tin (with or without an addition of tin crystals):

Red dyestuffs:

Benzo Purpurine 4 B, 4 B, 6 B, 10 B
Brilliant Congo G, R
Brilliant Geranine B, 3 B
Brilliant Purpurine R
Congo Red G, 4 R
Delta Purpurine 5 B, 7 B, G
Diamine Red B, 3 B
Geranine G, B B
Hessian Purple N (yellowish)
Rose Azurine B, G.

Orange dyestuffs:

Benzo Orange R
Brilliant Orange G
Chloramine Orange G
Congo Orange G, R
Mikado Orange 3 R, 4 R, 5 R
Toluylene Orange G (fairly good).

Yellow dyestuffs:

Chrysophenine
Curcumine W.

Green dyestuffs:

Benzo Green B B, G
Benzo Olive (fairly good).

Blue dyestuffs:

Azo Blue
Benzo Azurine G, 3 G, R
Benzo Blue 2 B, 3 B, B X, R W, 2 R, 4 R
Benzo Chrome Black Blue B
Benzo Cyanine B, 3 B, R
Benzo Dark Blue 3 B (β-Naphtol)
Benzo Indigo Blue (fairly good)
Benzo Sky Blue, 4 B
Benzo Red Blue G, R
Benzo Black Blue G, 5 G, R
Brilliant Azurine B, 5 G
Brilliant Benzo Blue 6 B
Brilliant Sulphon Azurine R
Congo Blue 2 B
Diazo Blue (β-Naphtol) (fairly good)
Diazo Blue 3 R (β-Naphtol)
Diazo Blue Black (undiazotised)
Diazo Indigo Blue B
Diazo Red Blue 3 R (β-Naphtol)
Diazo Black B, 3 B (undiazotised)
Diazo Black R, R extra (undiazotised)
Diazurine (β-Naphtol).

Violet dyestuffs:

Azo Violet
Benzo Violet R
Heliotrope
Heliotrope B B.

Brown dyestuffs:

Benzo Brown B, B X, N B X, B R, N B,
                    G G, R extra, N B R
Benzo Chrome Brown B, G, R, 3 R, 5 G
Benzo Dark Brown
Benzo Black Brown (yellowish)
Chloramine Brown G (yellowish)
Congo Corinth G, B
Congo Rubine
Direct Fast Brown B, G G
Diazo Brown G (yellowish)
Diazo Brilliant Black B (diazotised and
                    developed with soda)
Direct Bronze Brown
Mikado Brown G, B
Toluylene Brown B, B B O, M, R (fairly good).

Grey dyestuffs:

Benzo Chrome Black N (yellowish)
Benzo Fast Grey (yellowish)
Benzo Grey
Benzo Grey S extra
Diazo Black B H N
Pluto Black B, G, R.

Black dyestuffs:

Benzo Fast Black
Benzo Black
Benzo Black S extra
Benzo Black Blue
Diazo Brilliant Black B, R (β-Naphtol)
Diazo Black B, 3 B, B H N, R extra, R
                    (β-Naphtol yellowish)
Direct Blue Black B, N
Direct Deep Black E, E extra, R, G, T,
                    T N, R W (yellowish)
Pluto Black B, G, R.

Discharge Printing with Tin.

In discharging Benzidine dye-stuffs, acetate of tin can be used, with or without the addition of tin crystals.

The bleached cotton goods are previously dyed with the Benzidine colours (for unbleached goods less colouring matter is needed, but, of course, not such a good white is obtained) then dried, printed with white discharge, steamed for 5–10 minutes, or run through the Mather and Platt several times, then washed (in some cases treated with weak acid and washed) and dried. The lighter a dischargeable Benzidine dyestuffs is died, the easier it is to obtain a pure white, whereas the darker it is dyed, the more difficult it is to discharge. The strength of the discharge paste must be in proportion to the depth of shade and engraving of pattern. The more tin crystals are contained in discharge, the shorter time should the material be steamed, lest the cotton become tendered. The longer the goods are steamed the yellower the white becomes.

White Discharge I:

Boil: 4¾ galls. or 870 grms. acetate of tin 32° Tw.
   7 lbs. „ 110 „ wheat starch and
   1 pint „ 20 „ acetic acid 9° Tw. (30%).
     1000 grms.

White Discharge II:

Boil: 8½ lbs. or 138 grms. wheat starch
  1½ galls. „ 277 „ acetate of tin 32° Tw.
  7½ pints „ 170 „ gum water 1:1 and
  1¾ galls. „ 277 „ water, boil, and then add
   7 lbs. „ 111 „ tin crystals, whilst still lukewarm, and then
  1¾ lbs. „ 27 „ citric acid
    1000 grms.

Glycerine, acetine and a trace of Methylene Blue or Prussian Blue etc. are sometimes added to the white discharge. The latter colour prevents the discharged pieces from turning yellowish in course of time.

White discharge III is also very suitable for some dyestuffs and the discharge objects are not so liable to become yellow either in steaming or when the pieces are stocked.

White Discharge III:

F.

Boil: 2¾ lbs. or 90 grms. wheat starch
  2¼ galls. „ 720 „ water
  8¼ lbs. „ 270 „ white dextrine and
  9 lbs. 6 oz. „ 300 „ yellow prussiate of potash,
       then cool.

Dissolve: Z.

  18¾ lbs. or 600 grms. tin crystals in
  2⅛ galls. „ 750 „ gum water 1:1, and then add
  2¼ lbs. „ 72 „ powdered tartaric acid.
  When cold F is stirred into Z.

Steam for 5 minutes without pressure, then wash and dry.

These patterns were dyed for 1 hour at the boil with the addition of

$\frac{1}{4}$—1 lb. or $2\frac{1}{2}$—10 grms. Glauber's salt.

1—2 oz. „ 1—2 „ soda ash.

No. 1.
4 % Benzo Chrome Brown G.

No. 2.
2 % Brilliant Benzo Blue 6 B.

No. 3.
4 % Benzo Black Blue 5 G.

No. 4.
5 % Pluto Black B.

No. 5.
1 % Geranine G.

No. 6.
5 % Diazo Blue
      diazotised with:
    4 % nitrite
    10 % hydrochloric acid 20° Tw.
    developed with:
    4 % Developer A (β-Naphtol).

No. 7.
8 % Direct Blue Black B.

No. 8.
4 % Congo Corinth G.

No. 9.
5 % Brilliant Azurine B.

No. 10.
1 % Toluylene Brown G.

Nos. 2, 8, 9, 10, 11, 13 and 15—18 were discharged with White Discharge II.
Nos. 1, 3, 4, 5, 6, 7, 12 and 14 were discharged with White Discharge III.

Table 9.

Cotton Printing.

(Discharge Printing with tin).

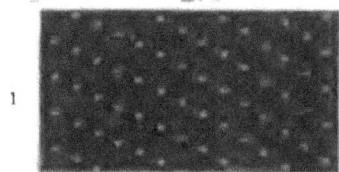

1

Dyed with: 4 . Benzo Chrome Brown G;
discharged with tin.

2

Dyed with: 2 . Brilliant Benzo Blue 6 B;
discharged with tin.

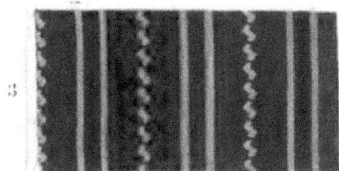

3

Dyed with: 4 . Benzo Black Blue 5 G;
discharged with tin.

4

Dyed with: 8 . Pluto Black B;
discharged with tin.

5

Dyed with: 1 . Geranine G;

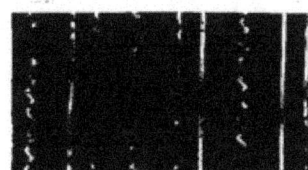

6

Dyed with: 5 . Diazo Blue Beta-Naphtol;
discharged with tin.

7

Dyed with: 8 . Direct Blue Black B;
discharged with tin.

8

Dyed with: 4 . Congo Corinth G

9

Dyed with: 5 . Brilliant Azurine B.

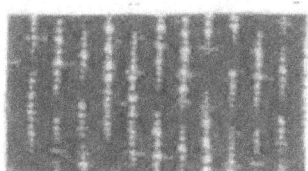

10

Dyed with: 4 . Toluylene Brown B.

FARBENFABRIKEN vorm. FRIEDR. BAYER & Co., ELBERFELD

Table 10.

Dyed as above:

No. 11.	No. 12.
2 % Congo Orange G.	4 % Benzo Chrome Brown B.

No. 13.	No. 14.
1 Benzo Fast Black.	$3^1{}_2$ % Benzo Green G.

No. 15.	No. 16.
2 % Chrysophenine.	4 % Benzo Chrome Brown R.

No. 17.	No. 18.
6 % Benzo Violet R.	5 % Benzo Purpurine 4 B.

No. 19.

Dyed with: 2 % **Brilliant** Azurine 5 G
discharged with: **White Discharge IV**
cover printed with: **Aniline** Black.

Aniline Black.

Boil:

2½ galls. or 400 grms.	water	
$3^1{}_4$ lbs. „	50 „	wheat starch
1 lb. $6^1{}_2$ oz. „	22.5 „	chlorate of potash
1 lb. 14 oz. „	30 „	yellow prussiate of potash, and when cold add
{ $7^1{}_2$ noggins „ { 3s „		aniline oil
{ $8^3{}_4$ noggins „ { 50 „		hydrochloric acid 27° Tw.

Steam for 5 minutes in the Mather & Platt, soap slightly, wash and dry.

White Discharge IV.

1 gall. or 196 grms.	tartrate of tin and ammonia discharge	
1 gall. „ 152 „	neutral thickening of starch tragacanth	
	348 grms.	

Tartrate of tin and ammonia discharge.

15 lbs. or 680 grms.	tin crystals dissolved in	
$1^1{}_2$ gall. „ 800 „	water, add slowly	
⅝ gall. „ 350 cc.	ammonia, allow to settle, run off the clear water which must be neutral, and then add cold	
$1^1{}_4$ galls. „ 900 grms.	tartrate of ammonia.	

Tartrate of ammonia.

Dissolve:

10 lbs. or 450 grms.	tartaric acid in	
1 gall. „ 150 „	hot water, and when lukewarm add	
$1^1{}_4$ galls. „ 540 cc.	ammonia, the solution must react alkaline.	

Cotton Printing.

Table 9.

(Discharge Printing with tin.)

11 — Dyed with: 2 Congo Orange G;
discharged with tin.

12 — Dyed with: 1 Benzo Chrome Brown B;
discharged with tin.

13 — Dyed with: 1 Benzo Fast Black;
discharged with tin.

14 — Dyed with: 3 Benzo Green G;
discharged with tin.

15 — Dyed with: 2 Chrysophenine;
discharged with tin.

16 — Dyed with: 1 Benzo Chrome Brown B;
discharged with tin.

17 — Dyed with: 6 Benzo Violet R;
discharged with tin.

18 — Dyed with: 5 Benzo Purpurine 4 B;
discharged with tin.

19 — Dyed with: 2 Brilliant Azurine 5 G; discharged with tin,
and cover printed with Aniline Black.

FARBENFABRIKEN vorm. FRIEDR. BAYER & Co., ELBERFELD.

Colour Discharge Printing with Tin.

The following undischargeable dyestuffs can be used with **tin crystals** for **coloured discharge** on Benzidine dyes.

Red dyestuffs:

Alizarine Red (alumina)
Brilliant Rhoduline Red B F
Pyronine G
Rhodamine S, B, G
Rhoduline Red G
Saffranine F F extra.

Yellow dyestuffs:

Auramine II
Persian Berry Extract (tin).

Green dyestuffs:

Brilliant Green.

Blue dyestuffs:

Chrome Blue (Chrome)
Celestine Blue B (Chrome)
Prussian Blue
Methylene Blue B B.

Violet dyestuffs:

Methyl Violet 2 B
Rhoduline Violet.

Table 11.

The dischargeable Benzidine colours can be colour discharged with tin crystals and undischargeable basic dyestuffs, as well as Extract of Persian Berries, lakes etc.

The following were dyed in an alkaline bath:

No. 1.

Dyed with: 4 % **Benzo Purpurine 4 B** on flannelette.

Green Discharge.

Boil:	5 oz.	or	20 grms.	**Brilliant Green crystals**
	19 oz.	„	75	„	wheat starch
	1¼ pints	„	105	„	water
	5¼ noggins	„	110	„	acetic acid 9° Tw. (30°/o)
	11¼ noggins	„	260	„	gum water 1 : 1, and then add
	2¼ pints	„	250	„	acetate of tin 32° Tw.
	2¼ oz.	„	10	„	tin crystals, and when cold add
	6¼ noggins	„	150	„	acetic acid tannic acid solution 1 : 1
	5 oz.	„	20	„	citric acid (powdered)

1000 grms.

No. 2.

Dyed with: 3 % **Benzo Blue RW** and after-treated with
1 % sulphate of copper for ¼ hour at the boil.

This treatment renders the blue very fast to light.

Persian Berry Yellow Discharge.

Discharged with:

2½ galls.	or	750 grms.	White Discharge II
			(see page 25)
7¼ noggs.	„	90	„	**Extract of Persian berries** 52° Tw.
3¼ pints	„	130	„	acetic acid thicken-
1 noggin	„	10	„	water [ing
¼ pint	„	20	„	acetic acid 9° Tw. (30°/o)

1000 grms.

No. 3.

Dyed with: 2 % **Congo Orange G.**

Violet Discharge.

Boil:	3 oz.	or	20 grms.	**Rhoduline Violet**
	7½ oz.	„	75	„	wheat starch
	¼ pint	„	100	„	acetic acid 9° Tw. (30 %)
	¼ pint	„	95	„	water
	1 pint	„	200	„	gum water 1 : 1 and
	4¼ noggs.	„	250	„	acetate of tin 32° Tw. and then add
	2 oz.	„	20	„	tin crystals
	7½ oz.	„	75	„	tannic acid dissolv- ed in
	1½ noggs.	„	75	„	acetic acid 9° Tw. (30 %)
	2 oz.	„	20	„	powdered citric acid

1000 grms.

No. 4.

Dyed with: 8 % **Direct Deep Black T.**

Green Discharge.

Boil:	¼ oz.	or	5 grms.	**Brilliant Green crystals**
	2½ oz.	„	25	„	**Auramine G**
	7¼ oz.	„	75	„	wheat starch
	½ pint	„	100	„	acetic acid 9° Tw. (30 %)
	¼ pint	„	95	„	water
	1 pint	„	260	„	gum water 1 : 1
	4¼ noggs.	„	250	„	acetate of tin 32° Tw.
	2 oz.	„	20	„	tin crystals, then add
	7½ oz.	„	75	„	tannic acid dissolv- ed in
	1¼ noggs.	„	75	„	acetic acid 9° Tw. (30 %)
	2 oz.	„	20	„	powdered citric acid

1000 grms.

No. 5.

Dyed with: 5 % **Diazo Blue.**
Diazotised with: 4 % nitrite, 10 % hydro-chloric acid 30° Tw.
Developed with: 4 % developer A (β-Naphtol)

Persian Berry Yellow Discharge.

2 galls.	or	700 grms.	White Discharge II
			(see page 25)
7½ noggs.	„	90	„	**Extract of Persian berries** 52° Tw.
4¼ pints	„	180	„	acetic acid thicken-
1 noggin	„	10	„	water [ing
¼ pint	„	20	„	acetic acid 9° Tw. (30 %)

1000 grms.

No. 6.

Dyed with: 1% **Brilliant Geranine B.**

Blue Discharge.

Boil:

1 oz.	or	10 grms.	Methyl Violet **6 B**
7½ oz.	..	75 ..	wheat starch
1¼ pints	..	250 ..	water
1 pint	..	200 ..	gum water 1 : 1, then add
¾ pint	..	200 ..	acetic acid 9° Tw. (30%)
1 noggin	..	50 ..	acetate of tin 32° Tw., then further add
7½ oz.	..	75 ..	tannic acid dissolved in
1½ noggs.	..	75 ..	acetic acid 9° Tw. (30%)
2 oz.	..	20 ..	powdered citric acid
		1000 grms.	

No. 7.

Dyed with: 1½% **Benzo Grey S extra.**

Pink Discharge.

Boil:

3 oz.	or	30 grms.	Rhodamine **6 G**
7½ oz.	..	75 ..	wheat starch
½ pint	..	100 ..	acetic acid 9° Tw. (30%)
2½ noggs	..	205 ..	water
1 pint	..	200 ..	gum water 1 : 1, then add
½ pint	..	100 ..	acetate of tin 32° Tw., and then add
7½ oz.	..	75 ..	tannic acid dissolved in
1½ noggs.	..	75 ..	acetic acid 9° Tw. (30%)
2 oz.	..	20 ..	powdered citric acid
		1000 grms.	

Green Discharge.

Boil:

2 oz.	or	20 grms.	Brilliant Green **crystals**
7½ oz.	..	75 ..	wheat starch
½ pint	..	100 ..	acetic acid 9° Tw. (30%)
1½ pints	..	315 ..	water
1 pint	..	200 ..	gum water 1 : 1, and then add
1 noggin	..	60 ..	acetate of tin 32° Tw.
7½ oz.	..	75 ..	tannic acid dissolved in
1½ noggs.	..	75 ..	acetic acid 9° Tw. (30%)
2 oz.	..	20 ..	powdered citric acid
		1000 grms.	

Persian Berry Yellow Discharge.

11½ noggs.	or	250 grms.	White discharge II (see page 25)
3½ noggs.	..	90 ..	Extract of Persian berries 32° Tw.
1 gallon	..	640 ..	acetic acid thickening
1 noggin	..	20 ..	acetic acid 9° Tw. (30%)
		1000 grms.	

No. 8.

Dyed with: 3% **Benzo Green G.**

Pink Discharge.

Boil:

3 oz.	or	30 grms.	**Rhodamine 6 G**
7½ oz.	..	75 ..	wheat starch
1 noggin	..	60 ..	water
½ pint	..	100 ..	acetic acid 9° Tw. (30%)
1 pint	..	200 ..	gum water 1 : 1
1¼ pint	..	250 ..	acetate of tin 32° Tw. and add
2½ oz.	..	25 ..	tin crystals, then
9 oz.	..	90 ..	tannic acid dissolved in
½ pint	..	90 ..	acetic acid 9° Tw. (30%)
2 oz.	..	20 ..	powdered citric acid
		1000 grms.	

Fast Black.

Printed with

3 pints	or	300 grms.	**Fast Black**
6½ pints	..	620 ..	acetic acid starch tragacanth thickening
2½ noggs.	..	80 ..	acetate of chrome 32° Tw.
		1000 grms.	

No. 9.

Dyed with: 3% Benzo Chrome Brown B and treated at the boil for ½ hour with
2% sulphate of copper
3% bichromate of potash.

Pink Discharge.

Discharged with: 30 grms. **Rhodamine 6 G** the same as No. 8.

Persian Berry Yellow Discharge.

5½ pints	or	500 grms.	White discharge II (see page 25)
3½ noggs.	..	90	Extract of Persian berries 32° Tw.
½ noggin	..	10 ..	water
1 noggin	..	25 ..	acetic acid 9° Tw. (30%)
1½ pints	..	380 ..	acetic acid thickening
		1000 grms.	

Cotton Printing.

(Coloured discharge printing with tin.)

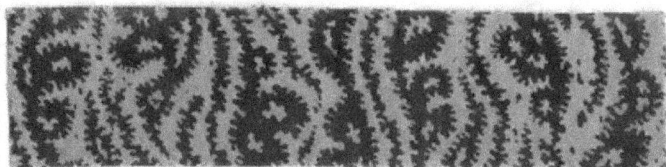

Table 11.

1 Dyed with: 4% Benzo Purpurine 4 B; discharged with: 2% Brilliant Green.

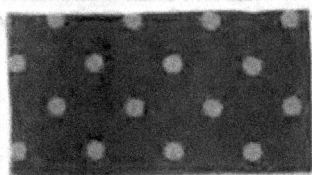

2 Dyed with: 3% Benzo Blue RW (coppered); discharged with: Persian berry Yellow discharge.

3 Dyed with: 2% Congo Orange G; discharged with: 3% Rhoduline Violet.

4 Dyed with: 8% Direct Deep Black T; discharged with: 2.5% Auramine G. 0.5% Brilliant Green crystals.

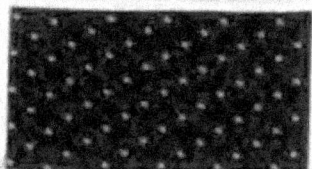

5 Dyed with: 3% Diazo Blue (Beta Naphtol); discharged with: Persian berry Yellow discharge.

6 Dyed with: 1% Brilliant Geranine B; discharged with: 1% Methyl Violet 6 B.

7 Dyed with: 1% Benzo Grey S extra; discharged with: 3% Rhodamine 6 G. 2% Brilliant Green. Persian berry Yellow discharge.

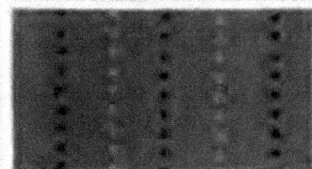

8 Dyed with: 3% Benzo Green G; discharged with: 3% Rhodamine 6 G; printed with: 30% Fast Black.

9 Dyed with: 3% Benzo Chrome Brown B; discharged with: 3% Rhodamine 5 G. Persian berry Yellow discharge.

FARBENFABRIKEN vorm. FRIEDR. BAYER & Co. ELBERFELD.

No. 10.

Dyed with: 6 % **Benzo Chrome Black Blue B.**

Red Discharge.

Boil:

7½ oz.	or	60	grms.	**Rhodamine 6 G**
1 oz.	„	8	„	**Auramine II**
9½ oz.	„	75	„	wheat starch
3¾ noggs.	„	132	„	acetic acid 9° Tw. (30 %)
¾ noggin	„	25	„	water
1¾ noggs.	„	80	„	gum water 1:1, and then add
5¾ noggs.	„	250	„	acetate of tin 32° Tw.
3½ oz.	„	30	„	tin crystals
1½ pints	„	320	„	acetic acid tannic acid solution 1:1
2½ oz.	„	20	„	powdered citric acid
		1000	grms.	

White Discharge.

1 gall. or 1000 grms. **White discharge II** (see page 25)

3 noggs. „ 100 „ **glycerine** 48° Tw.

No. 11.

Dyed with: 4 % **Benzo Brown GG.**

Green Discharge.

Boil:

2 oz.	or	20	grms.	**Brilliant Green crystals**
7½ oz.	„	75	„	wheat starch
1 pint	„	200	„	gum water 1:1
½ pint	„	100	„	acetic acid 9° Tw. (30 %)
2½ noggs.	„	125	„	water
1¼ pints	„	250	„	acetate of tin 32° Tw.
7½ oz.	„	75	„	tannic acid dissolved in
1½ noggs.	„	75	„	acetic acid 9° Tw. (30 %)
2 oz.	„	20	„	powdered citric acid
		1000	grms.	

No. 12.

Dyed with: 3 % **Heliotrope B B.**

Green Discharge.

Boil:

½ oz.	or	5	grms.	**Brilliant Green crystals**
2½ oz.	„	25	„	**Auramine G**
7½ oz.	„	75	„	wheat starch
1 pint	„	200	„	gum water 1:1
½ pint	„	100	„	acetic acid 9° Tw. (30 %)
1¼ pints	„	215	„	water
1½ noggs.	„	90	„	acetate of tin 32° Tw.
7½ oz.	„	75	„	tannic acid dissolved in
1½ noggs.	„	75	„	acetic acid 9° Tw. (30 %)
2 oz.	„	20	„	powdered citric acid
		1000	grms.	

White Discharge.

White discharge II (see page 25).

No. 13.

Dyed with: 4 % **Brilliant Azurine 5 G** afterwards treated with 1 % sulphate of copper for ½ hour at the boil.

Discharged with: **Persian berry Yellow discharge** the same as No. 2 (see page 31).

Printed with: **Fast Black** the same as No. 8 (see page 32).

Cotton Printing.

Table 12.

(Coloured discharges with tin.)

10

Dyed with: 6 Benzo Chrome Black
Blue B; discharged with: 6 Rhodamine
6 G and 0,8 Auramine II and for
White with acetate of tin.

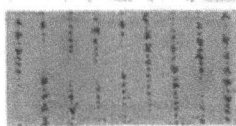

11

Dyed with: 4 Benzo Brown G G;
discharged with:
2 Brilliant Green crystals.

12

Dyed with: 3 Heliotrope B B;
discharged with: 2 Auramine G,
1 Brilliant Green and for White with
tin crystals.

13

Dyed with: 4 Benzo Azurine 3 G cop-
pered; discharged with: Persian berry
Yellow discharge; cover printed with:
Fast Black.

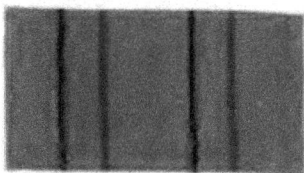

14

Dyed with: 3 Benzo Blue 2 B;
discharged with: 2 Saffranine FF extra,
1 Auramine G;
cover printed with: Fast Black.

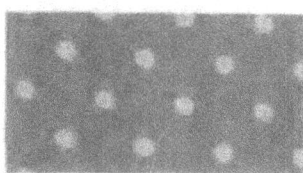

15

Dyed with: 3 Yellow P R. 0,1 Poly-
lene Orange G. 0,8 Benzo Sky Blue;
discharged with: tin crystals.

16

Dyed with: 4 Azo Violet;
discharged with: 3 Auramine II.

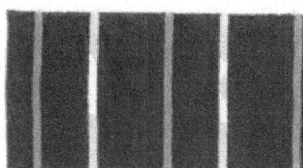

17

Dyed with: 3 Benzo Azurine 3 G;
discharged with:
Persian berry Yellow discharge
and for White with tin crystals.

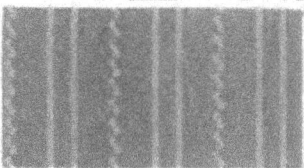

18

Dyed with: 4 Benzo Sky Blue;
discharged with:
Persian berry Yellow discharge.

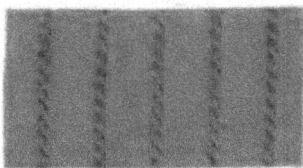

19

Dyed with: 4 Benzo Fast Black;
discharged with:
2 Brilliant Rhoduline Red B D in paste.

FARBENFABRIKEN vorm. FRIEDR. BAYER & Co., ELBERFELD.

No. 14.

Dyed with: 5% Benzo Blue 2 B.

Red Discharge.

Boil:

2 oz. or	20 grms.	**Saffranine F F** extra
1 oz.	„	10	„	**Auramine G**
7½ oz.	„	75	„	wheat starch
1 pint	„	260	„	gum water 1 : 1
1½ pint	„	115	„	water
1½ pint	„	100	„	acetic acid 9° Tw. (30 %)
1¼ pints	„	250	„	acetate of tin 32° Tw.
				and then add
7½ oz.	„	75	„	tannic acid
1½ noggs.	„	75	„	acetic acid 9° Tw. (30 %)
2 oz.	„	20	„	citric acid crystals
	1000 grms.		

No. 16.

Dyed with: 4 % **Azo Violet.**

Yellow Discharge.

Boil:

3 oz. or	30 grms.	**Auramine II**
7½ oz.	„	75	„	wheat starch
1 pint	„	260	„	gum water 1 : 1
1½ pint	„	110	„	water
1½ pint	„	100	„	acetic acid 9° Tw. (30 %)
1¼ pint	„	250	„	acetate of tin 32° Tw.
				and then add
1½ oz.	„	5	„	tin crystals
7½ oz.	„	75	„	tannic acid dissolved in
1½ noggs.	„	75	„	acetic acid 9° Tw. (30 %)
2 oz.	„	20	„	powdered citric acid
	1000 grms.		

No. 18.

Dyed with: 1 % **Benzo Sky Blue.**

Persian Berry Yellow Discharge.

13½ pints or 600 grms. White discharge II (see page 25)

7½ noggs.	„	90	„	**Extract of Persian berries** 52° Tw.
2 noggs.	„	20	„	acetic acid 9° Tw. (30 %)
1 nogg.	„	10	„	water
7 pints	„	280	„	acetic acid thickening
	1000 grms.		

No. 15.

Dyed with: 5% Yellow P R
0.1 % Toluylene Orange G
0.5 % Benzo Sky Blue.

Discharged with: White discharge II (see page 25).

Toluylene Orange G and Benzo Sky Blue are dischargeable with tin crystals, whereas Paraline Yellow being undischargeable remains.

No. 17.

Dyed with: 5 % **Benzo** Azurine 3 G.

White discharge II (page 25) reduced 1 W.

Persian Berry Yellow Discharge.

13½ noggs. or 150 grms. White discharge II (see page 25)

7½ noggs.	„	90	„	**Extract of Persian berries** 52° Tw.
1 noggin	„	10	„	water
2½ galls.	„	730	„	acetic acid thickening
2 noggs.	„	20	„	acetic acid 9° Tw. (30 %)
	1000 grms.		

No. 19.

Dyed with: 1 % Benzo **Fast Black.**

Red Discharge.

Boil:

2 oz. or	20 grms.	**Brilliant** Rhoduline Red **B D in paste**
7½ oz.	„	75	„	wheat starch
1 pint	„	260	„	gum water 1 : 1
1 pint	„	260	„	acetic acid 9° Tw. (30 %)
1 pint	„	260	„	water
1½ noggs.	„	70	„	acetate of tin 32° Tw.
				and then add
7½ oz.	„	75	„	tannic acid dissolved in
1½ noggs.	„	75	„	acetic acid 9° Tw. (30 %)
2 oz.	„	20	„	powdered citric acid
	1000 grms.		

The pieces printed with discharge colours are steamed for 10 mins. and passed through a bath of tartar emetic, then washed and dried.

(Colour discharge printing with tint)

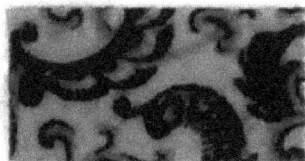

20

Dyed with: Benzo Purpurine 4 B; discharged with: Persian Berry Yellow and Methyl Violet.

21

Dyed with: Benzo Sky Blue; discharged with: Methyl Violet.

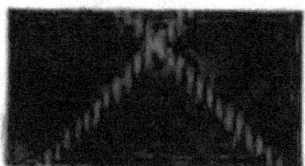

22

Dyed with: Diazo Black B; discharged with: Brilliant Green, Persian Berry Yellow and Auramine.

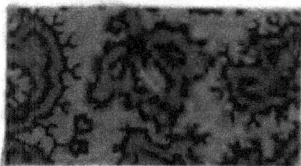

23

Dyed with: Benzo Purpurine 10 B; discharged with: Brilliant Green.

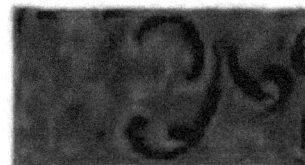

24

Dyed with: Benzo Brown N G; discharged with: Persian Berry Yellow and Brilliant Green.

25

Dyed with: Benzo Olive and Benzo Black Blue 5 G; discharged with: Methyl Violet and Persian Berry Yellow.

26

Dyed with: Heliotrope B B and Geranine G; discharged with: Persian Berry Yellow and Methyl Violet.

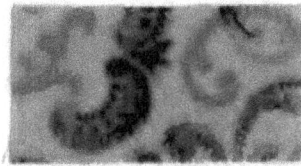

27

Dyed with: Benzo Purpurine 4 B; discharged with: Methyl Violet, Brilliant Green, Persian Berry Yellow.

28

Dyed with: Benzo Brown N B and Geranine G; discharged with: Methylene Blue and Brilliant Green.

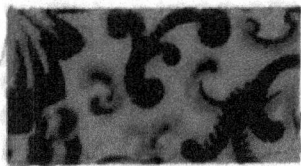

29

Dyed with: Benzo Sky Blue; discharged with: Persian Berry Yellow and Methyl Violet.

FARBENFABRIKEN vorm. FRIEDR. BAYER & Co., ELBERFELD.

Table 14

No. 30.

Dyed with:
  1 °₀ **Benzo Cyanine 3 B**
  ¹∕₂ °₀ **Chrysophenine.**
Discharged with:
  tin-discharge
  Brilliant Green crystals.
Printed with:
  Steam Black.

No. 31.

Printed with:
  1¹∕₄ °₀ Benzo Purpurine 10 B
  ¹∕₄ °₀ Geranine **B B**
  ¹∕₂ °₀ **Benzo Purpurine 4 B.**
Discharged with:
  Brilliant Green crystals.

No. 32.

Dyed with:
  1¹∕₂ °₀ **Benzo Cyanine 3 B**
  0,50 °₀ **Diazo Black B.**
Discharged with:
  Persian **Berry Yellow**
  Brilliant **Green crystals.**
Printed with:
  Steam **Black.**

No. 33.

Dyed with:
  3 °₀ **Benzo Purpurine 4 B.**
Discharged with:
  Methylene Blue
  Brilliant Green crystals.
Printed with:
  Logwood Black.

No. 34.

Dyed with:
  1 °₀ **Benzo Cyanine 3 B**
  0,64 °₀ **Chrysophenine.**
Discharged with:
  Brilliant Green crystals.

No. 35.

Dyed with:
  3 °₀ Benzo **Purpurine 4 B.**
Discharged with:
  Methylene Blue.

Table 11.

Cotton Printing.
(Coloured discharges with tin).

Dyed with: Benzo Cyanin 4B and Chrysophenine; discharged with: tin discharge (for white), Brilliant Green; printed with: Steam Black.

Dyed with: Benzo Purpurine 10B, Geranine BB, Benzo Purpurine 4B; discharged with: Brilliant Green crystals.

Dyed with: Benzo Cyanine 3B, Diazo Black B; discharged with: Persian Berry Yellow, Brilliant Green; printed with: Steam Black.

Dyed with: Benzo Purpurine 4B; discharged with: Methylene Blue, Brilliant Green; printed with: Logwood Black.

Dyed with: Benzo Cyanine 3B and Chrysophenine; discharged with: Brilliant Green crystals.

Dyed with: Benzo Purpurine 4B; discharged with: Methylene Blue.

FARBENFABRIKEN verm. FRIEDR. BAYER & Co., ELBERFELD.

When dyed on cotton the following Benzidine dyestuffs **cannot be discharged with acetate of tin.**

Red Dyestuffs:

Yellow P R (developed).

Yellow Dyestuffs:

Chloramine Yellow
Curcumine S
Direct Yellow R
Mikado Yellow G
Yellow P R
Thiazole Yellow.

Brown and Claret Dystuffs:

Benzo Brown 5 R (turns yellow)
Diazo Bordeaux (developer A)
Hessian Brown B
Katigene Black Brown
Yellow P R with developer B (turns yellow).

Black Dyestuffs:

Benzo Chrome Black, after chromed (reddish brown).
Diazo Black H (turns yellow).

Discharge Printing with Zinc powder.

Dyed on cotton the following Benzidine colours can be discharged with zinc powder:

Red Dyestuffs:

Benzo Purpurine 1 B, 4 B, 6 B, 10 B
Brilliant Congo G, R
Brilliant Geranine B, 3 B
Brilliant Purpurine R
Congo Red, G, G R, 4 R
Delta Purpurine 5 B, 7 B, G
Diamine Red B, 3 B
Geranine G, B B
Hessian Brilliant Purple B
Hessian Purple N, B, N B (yellow)
Rose Azurine B, G.

Orange Dyestuffs:

Benzo Orange R
Brilliant Orange G
Chloramine Orange G
Congo Orange G, R
Mikado Orange 2 R, 3 R, 4 R, 5 R, G O, G,
    R, R O, 2 R O, 3 R O, 4 R, 5 R O.
Toluylene Orange G.

Yellow Dyestuffs:

Chrysamine G, R, R S, G S
Chrysophenine
Curcumine S, W
Direct Yellow R (fairly well)
Hessian Yellow
Mikado Yellow.

Green Dyestuffs:

Benzo Dark Green
Benzo Green B B, G
Benzo Olive (fairly good).

Blue Dyestuffs:

Azo Blue
Benzo Azurine G, 3 G, R
Benzo Black Blue G, 5 G, R
Benzo Blue B X, 2 B, 3 B, R W, 2 R, 4 R
Benzo Chrome Black Blue B
Benzo Cyanine B, 3 B, R
Benzo Indigo Blue
Benzo Navy Blue B
Benzo Red Blue G, R
Benzo Sky Blue, 4 B
Brilliant Azurine B, 5 G
Brilliant Benzo Blue 6 B
Brilliant Sulphon Azurine R
Chicago Blue B, R
Congo Blue 2 B
Diazo Black B, 3 B, R, R extra (undiazotised)

Diazo Blue (β-Naphtol)
Diazo Blue 3 R (β-Naphtol).
Diazo Blue Black (undiazotised)
Diazo Navy Blue 3 B (β-Naphtol)
Diazo Indigo Blue B
Diazo Red Blue 3 R (β-Naphtol)
Diazurine B (β-Naphtol).

Violet Dyestuffs:

Azo Violet
Benzo Violet R
Diazo Violet R (β-Naphtol).
Heliotrope (fairly good)
Heliotrope B B

Brown Dyestuffs:

Benzo Brown B, B X, N B X, B R, N B,
    G G, R extra, N B R.
Benzo Chrome Brown G, B, R, 3 R, 5 G
Benzo Dark Brown
Benzo Black Brown
Chloramine Brown G
Congo Rubine
Diazo Brown G
Diazo Brilliant Black B (diazotised and
    developed with soda)
Direct Bronze Brown
Direct Fast Brown G G, B
Hessian Brown B
Mikado Brown B, G
Toluylene Brown B, B B O, M, R.

Grey Dyestuffs:

Benzo Chrome Black N
Benzo Fast Grey
Benzo Grey
Benzo Grey S extra
Diazo Black B H N
Pluto Black B, G, R.

Black Dyestuffs:

Benzo Fast Black
Benzo Black, S extra
Diazo Brilliant Black B, R (β-Naphtol)
Diazo Blue Black (β-Naphtol)
Diazo Black B, 3 B, R, B H N, R extra
    (β-Naphtol)
Direct Blue Black B, N
Direct Deep Black E, E extra, G, R, T, R W
Pluto Black B, G, R.

Zinc powder with bisulphite of soda is a more powerful discharge than acetate of tin. In order to prevent the rollers and doctors from being affected, only the finest sifted zinc powder should be used. The discharge paste must be printed on with a brush, in order to prevent the zinc powder from "sticking in" the engraving.

After printing, steam for 1 hour without pressure, wash, if necessary in a slightly acid bath, wash and dry.

White Discharge.

12', lbs. or 333 grms. zinc powder, well sifted, and

1 gallon „ 333 „ gum water 1:1 grind well, then cool down
with ice and add gradually

7'' pints „ 334 „ sodium bisulphite 66° Tw.
1000 grms.

Occasionally glycerine, ammonia, soda etc. are added to the discharge.

For dyeing directions see page 22.

| No. 1. | No. 2. |
| 6°₀ Benzo Chrome Black Blue B. | 4°₀ Azo Violet. |

| No. 3. | No. 4. |
| 5°₀ Benzo Brown B X. | 5°₀ Brilliant Purpurine R. |

| No. 5. | No. 6. |
| 2¹,°₀ Congo Orange R. | 3°₀ Benzo Cyanine B. |

| No. 7. | No. 8. |
| 3°₀ Benzo Olive. | 8°₀ Pluto Black B. |

| No. 9. | No. 10. |
| 1 ° Benzo Fast Grey | 2°₀ Chrysophenine. |

Table 15

Cotton Printing.
(Discharges with zinc powder.)

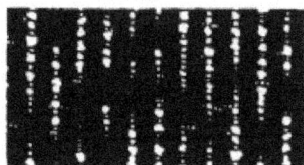

1

Dyed with: 6% Benzo Chrome Black
Blue B; discharged with zinc powder.

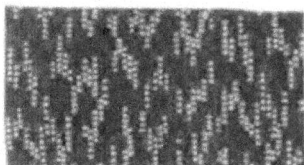

2

Dyed with: 4% Azo Violet;
discharged with zinc powder.

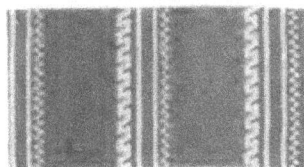

3

Dyed with: 5% Benzo Brown BX,
discharged with zinc powder.

4

Dyed with: 5% Brilliant Purpurine R;
discharged with zinc powder.

5

Dyed with: 2% Congo Orange R;
discharged with zinc powder.

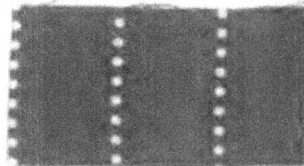

6

Dyed with: 3% Benzo Cyanine R;
discharged with zinc powder.

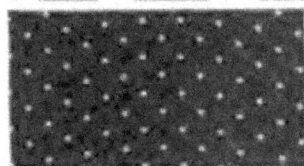

7

Dyed with: 3% Benzo Olive;
discharged with zinc powder.

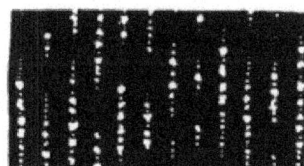

8

Dyed with: 8% Pluto Black B;
discharged with zinc powder.

9

Dyed with: 4% Benzo Fast Grey;
discharged with zinc powder.

10

Dyed with: 2% Chrysophenine;
discharged with zinc powder.

FARBENFABRIKEN vorm. FRIEDR. BAYER & Co., ELBERFELD.

When dyed on cotton the following Benzidine colours **cannot be discharged with zinc powder:**

Red Dyestuffs:

Yellow P R (developed).

Yellow Dyestuffs:

Chloramine Yellow
Curcumine S
Yellow P R
Thiazole Yellow.

Brown Dyestuffs:

Katigene Black Brown.

Black Dyestuffs:

Benzo Chrome Black.

The following dyestuffs are suitable for **coloured discharges** with **zinc powder** on Benzidine colours:

Red Dyestuffs:

Brilliant Rhodaline Red B D
Yellow P R (developed)
Rhoduline Red G
Saffranine F F extra.

Yellow Dyestuffs:

Yellow P R.

It can be discharged with:

1 lb. or 100 grms.	**Yellow P R**
2 lbs. „ 200 „	dextrine
3½ pints „ 400 „	water
2⅖ lbs. „ 240 „	zinc powder
1⅘ lbs. „ 180 „	bisulphite of soda 52° Tw.
4 oz. „ 24 „	glycerine 48° Tw.
3 oz. „ 16 „	ammonia.

Steam, sour, wash and dry.

In order to obtain a Red instead of a Yellow it can be diazotised and developed with β-Naphtol Developer.

Blue Dyestuffs:

Methylene Blue B B.

The following recipe can be used for discharging:

Dissolve:

10 oz. or 10 grms.	**Saffranine F F extra** in
3 pints „ 60 „	water and warm with
1½ galls. „ 300 „	gum water 1:1, and then add
18⅘ lbs. „ 300 „	zinc powder; when cooled down add
11 pints „ 300 „	sodium bisulphite 72° Tw.
15 oz. „ 15 „	tannic acid dissolved in
3 noggins „ 15 „	acetic acid 9° Tw. (30 %)
	1000 grms.

Steam for ¼ hour without pressure, then run through a bath of tartar emetic, wash and dry.

Coloured Discharges

with oxidizing agents.

Most of the Benzidine dyestuffs can be discharged with oxidizing agents (such as chlorates etc.) but a few of them withstand the same. These can be employed for coloured discharges in dischargeable dyestuffs such as Indigo, Alizarine, Chrome, Diamond and Basic Colours. This small selection of colours withstanding the action of chlorine to a more or less degree can be used as coloured resists for the Aniline Black discharge style.

The following Benzidine colours, which entirely or partly resist oxidizing agents, are specially adapted for **coloured discharges** on Indigo, Alizarine colours fixed on chrome, Basic colours etc. **with** the aid of **oxidizing agents**; they can also be employed as discharges on Aniline Black by the ferrocyanide process:

Red Dyestuffs:

Benzo Fast Red
Brilliant Geranine B
Geranine G.

Orange Dyestuffs:

Chloramine Orange G
Congo Orange G R
Mikado Orange.

Yellow Dyestuffs:

Chloramine Yellow
Chrysophenine.

Blue Dyestuffs:

Benzo Sky Blue.

Brown Dyestuffs:

All the Benzo Browns.

These Benzidine dyestuffs not affected by chlorine are also used for discharging dyed Indigo Blues:

No. 1.

Yellow Discharge.

Boil:

7¼ pints	or 400 grms.	chlorate of soda solution 76° Tw. (16¼ lbs. per gallon or 500 grms. : 300 grms. water)	
{ 4¼ lbs.	or 148 grms.	China clay	
{ 1 pint	„ 40 „	water	
¾ lb.	„ 24 „	**Chrysophenine** and	
5¼ lbs.	„ 180 „	British gum, and then add	
10 oz.	„ 20 „	red prussiate of potash, and when cold add	
{ 1¼ lbs.	„ 40 „	citric acid dissolved in	
{ 2½ pints	„ 100 „	water.	

No. 2.

Orange Discharge.

Boil:

7¼ pints	or 400 grms.	chlorate of soda solution 76° Tw. (16¼ lbs. per gallon or 500 grms. : 300 grms. water)
{ 4¼ lbs.	„ 148 grms.	China clay
{ 1 pint	„ 40 „	water
1 lb.	„ 32 „	**Chloramine Orange G** and
5¼ lbs.	„ 180 „	British gum, and then add
10 oz.	„ 20 „	red prussiate of potash, and when cold add
{ 1¼ lbs.	„ 40 „	citric acid dissolved in
{ 2½ pints	„ 100 „	water.

White Discharge.

Boil:

7¼ pints	or 400 grms.	chlorate of soda
{ 4¼ lbs.	„ 148 „	China clay
{ 1¾ pints	„ 72 „	water
5¼ lbs.	„ 180 „	British gum, and then add
4¼ pints	„ 20 „	red prussiate of potash, and when cold, add
{ 1¼ lbs.	„ 40 „	citric acid dissolved in
{ 2½ pints	„ 100 „	water.

Steam for ¼–½ hour without pressure, and then wash and dry.

No. 3.

Padded with:

7½ oz.	or 15 grms.	**Alizarine Viridine in paste**
2½ pints	„ 100 „	mucilage of tragacanth 65 : 1000
3¼ pints	„ 129 „	water
15 pints	„ 600 „	water
½ noggin	„ 6 „	acetate of chrome 32° Tw.
2½ pints	„ 100 „	water
1¼ pints	„ 50 „	acetic acid 9° Tw. (30 %)
	1000 grms.	

Printed with:

4 lbs. 11 oz.	or 300 grms.	**Alizarine Viridine in paste**
6½ pints	„ 620 „	acetic acid starch tragacanth thickening
3½ noggs.	„ 80 „	acetate of chrome 32° Tw.
	1000 grms.	

Discharged with:

Boil:

8¼ oz.	or 33 grms.	Chloramine **Yellow**
5½ lbs.	„ 350 „	British gum
2 lbs.	„ 125 „	chlorate of soda and
4⅓ pints	„ 332 „	water, and when luke warm add
2½ oz.	„ 10 grms.	red prussiate of potash, and when cold add
1½ pints	„ 150 „	citrate of soda 52° Tw.

Steam for one hour without pressure, soap wash and dry.

No. 4.

Padded with:

Dissolve:

{ 12½ oz.	or 25 grms.	**Alizarine Bordeaux BP** 20 % in
{ 1⅛ pints	„ 45 „	ammonia spc. gravity 0.950
{ ¾ nogg.	„ 10 „	glycerine 48° Tw.
{ 5 pints	„ 200 „	water, and then add
15 pints	„ 600 „	water
{ 1¾ noggs.	„ 20 „	acetate of chrome 32° Tw.
{ 2½ pints	„ 100 „	water.

Yellow Discharge.

Boil:

1 lb.	or 33 grms.	**Chloramine Yellow**
6 lbs.	„ 192 „	British gum
6¼ pints	„ 247 „	water
½ lb.	„ 16 „	chlorate of potash, and
½ lb.	„ 17 „	chlorate of soda, allow to cool down a little, and then add
5 lbs. 2 oz.	„ 165 grms.	powdered red prussiate of potash (sifted) and when cold, add
7 pints	„ 330 grms.	citrate of soda 38° Tw.
	1000 grms.	

Steam for 1 hour without pressure, soap for 3 mins. at 86° Faht. wash full width, nip through, mangle and dry. The soaping, washing and squeezing must take place "open" (not in the rope) as in the latter case "marking off" is liable to occur. The goods can also be hydro-extracted.

No. 5.

Padded with:

1¾ oz. or	70 grms.	Brilliant Alizarine Blue D in paste
3¾ pints „	2000 „	water
1¼ pints „	1000 „	mucilage of tragacanth 65 : 1000
7¼ pints „	5770 „	water
¼ noggin „	60 „	acetate of chrome 32° Tw.
3½ noggs. „	1100 „	hyposulphite of soda solution 80 : 20 water
	10000 grms.	

Discharged with:

Boil:

1 lb. or	23 grms.	Geranine G
6 lbs. „	138 „	British gum
11 pints „	434 „	water
3 oz. „	6 „	chlorate of soda
3 oz. „	6 „	chlorate of potash
1¼ lbs. „	40 „	powdered red prussiate of potash, and when cold, add
4¼ noggs. „	50 grms.	citrate of soda 52° Tw.
5 pints „	231 „	starch tragacanth thickening
	1000 grms.	

No. 6.

Padded with:

3lbs. 2oz. or	50 grms.	Alizarine Cyanine Black G in paste
2¼ pints „	45 „	ammonia 0.950
1¼ noggs. „	10 „	glycerine 48° Tw.
8¾ pints „	175 „	water
2¾ galls. „	600 „	water
3¼ noggs. „	20 „	acetate of chrome 32° Tw.
5 pints „	100	water.
	1000 grms.	

Discharged with:

Boil:

1 lb. or	33 grms.	Congo Orange G
6 lbs. „	138 „	British gum
11 pints „	435 „	water
3¼ oz. „	7 „	chlorate of potash
3¼ oz. „	7 „	chlorate of soda, and then add
1¼ lbs. „	40 „	powdered red prussiate of potash, and when cold add
4¼ noggs. „	50 grms.	citrate of soda 38° Tw.
5 pints „	226 „	starch tragacanth thickening
	1000 grms.	

Striking effects can be produced by combining mordant dyestuffs and Benzidine colours which are dischargeable by chlorates.

No. 7.

Padded with:

10 oz. or	20 grms.	Alizarine Bordeaux B P 20%
1½ pints „	45 „	ammonia 0.950
½ nogg „	10 „	glycerine 48° Tw.
5 pints „	200 „	water
12½ pints „	500 „	water
1½ noggs. „	20 „	acetate of chrome 32° Tw.
2½ pints „	100 „	water
2½ oz. „	5 „	Chrysophenine
2½ pints „	100 „	water
	1000 grms.	

Discharged with:

White Discharge F.

Boil:

5 lbs. or	400 grms.	British gum
18 oz. „	180 „	chlorate of soda and
3¾ pints „	330 „	water, and then add
2 oz. „	10 „	powdered red prussiate of potash and when cold, add
1¼ noggs. „	150 „	citrate of soda 52° Tw.
	1000 grms.	

The process depends on Alizarine Bordeaux being discharged with chlorates, whereas Chrysophenine is not destroyed, and thus yellow figures may be produced on a brown ground.

(Colour discharge printing with oxidising agents.)

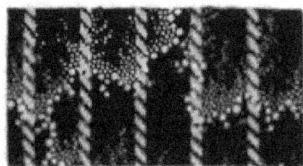

1 — Indigo discharged with Chrysophenine.

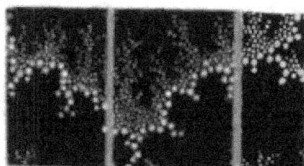

2 — Indigo discharged with Chloramine Orange G.

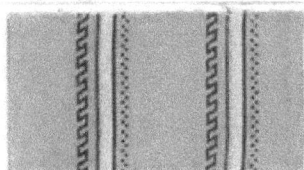

3 — Alizarine Viridine discharged with Chrysophenine.

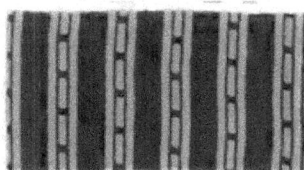

4 — Alizarine Bordeaux R P discharged with Chloramine Yellow.

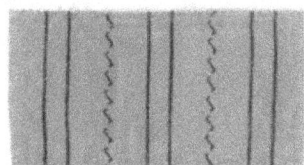

5 — Brilliant Alizarine Blue D discharged with Geranine G.

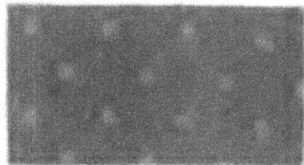

6 — Alizarine Cyanine Black G discharged with Congo Orange G.

7 — Alizarine Bordeaux R P and Chrysophenine discharged with chlorate of soda.

8 — Alizarine Bordeaux R P and Geranine G discharged with chlorate of soda.

9 — Brilliant Alizarine Blue S P and Geranine G discharged with acetate of tin.

10 — Aniline Black discharged with Congo Orange G.

FARBENFABRIKEN vorm. FRIEDR. BAYER & Co., ELBERFELD.

Table 16

No. 8.

Similar effects to No. 7 are obtained with Geranine G which is fairly resistant to the action of chlorine.

Padded with:

The same as in No. 7 but instead of
5 grms. Chrysophenine take
5 „ **Geranine G.**

Discharged with:

White Discharge F

same as in No. 7.

Steam for 1 hour without pressure, run through a weak soap bath, wash and dry. In this way a pink on a brown ground is produced.

No. 9.

Padded with:

}	4 oz. or	40 grms.	**Brilliant Alizarine Blue S P** dissolved in		
}	1 pint „	200 „	water, thickened with		
}	¾ pint „	100 „	mucilage of tragacanth 65 : 1000		
}	1½ pint „	350 „	water		
}	1½ noggs „	100 „	acetate of chrome 32° Tw.		
}	½ pint „	100 „	water, and then add		
}	½ oz. „	5 „	Geranine **G** dissolved in		
}	½ pint „	35 „	water.		
		1285 grms.			

Discharged with:

White Discharge II reduced 2 and 1 page 25.

Steam for 1 hour without pressure, wash, soap slightly if requisite, wash and then dry.

If Geranine G, which is discharged by tin, is combined with Brilliant Alizarine Blue S P, which is not discharged, and then printed with acetate of tin and steamed, Geranine G alone is discharged, and the light blue of Brilliant Alizarine Blue S P remains.

Discharge Printing on Aniline Black.

Table 17.

No. 11.

The following colours can be printed on white calico and steamed for ¹₂ hour:

Pink Discharge.

.	15 oz. or	15 grms.	Geranine G
3¹₂ pints	„	65	„ water
11¹₄ lbs.	„	180	„ zinc white
11 pints	„	220	„ mucilage of tragacanth 65 : 1000
8³₄ pints	„	220	„ gum water 1 : 1
1¹₂ pints	„	30	„ glycerine 48° Tw.
1¹₂ pints	„	30	„ olive oil

Slop pad with Ferrocyanide Aniline Black, dry, oxidise in Mather and Platt, then run through a bath of silicate of soda, wash and dry.

No. 12.

Padded with Ferrocyanide Aniline Black, dried, and then discharged with:

Yellow Discharge.

Boil:			
	12 oz. or	12 grms.	Chloramine Yellow
15 pints	„	306	„ water
12¹₂ pints	„	250	„ mucilage of tragacanth 65 : 1000
1¹₄ galls.	„	250	„ starch tragacanth thickening
1¹₄ lbs.	„	20	„ phosphate of soda; when luke warm add
9³₄ lbs.	„	150	„ acetate of soda
2¹₄ noggs.	„	15	„ caustic soda 66° Tw.
		1000 grms..	

Steam for 5 mins. in Mather and Platt, run through a bath of silicate of soda, wash and dry.

No. 13.

Blue Discharge.

1¹₄ lbs. or	20 grms.	Benzo Sky Blue
3 pints	„ 60	„ water
11¹₄ lbs.	„ 180	„ zinc white
15 pints	„ 300	„ mucilage of tragacanth 65 : 1000
8³₄ pints	„ 220	„ gum water 1 : 1
1¹₄ pints	„ 30	„ glycerine 48° Tw.
1¹₂ pints	„ 30	„ olive oil
³₄ pint	„ 20	„ bisulphite of soda 66° Tw.

No. 14.

Red Discharge.

Boil:			
2 lbs. 2 oz. or	195 grms.	Benzo Purpurine 4 B
7¹₂ noggs.	155	„ water
12¹₂ noggs.	250	„ mucilage of tragacanth 65 : 1000
3 pints	„ 250	„ starch tragacanth thickening, and then add
5 oz.	„ 20	„ phosphate of soda, and when cold add
³₁₆ noggin	„ 15	„ caustic soda 66° Tw.
1¹₂ noggin	„ 30	„ bisulphite of soda 66° Tw.

Print on padded Aniline Black, steam for 5 mins., run through a bath of silicate of soda, wash and dry.

Table 17

Aniline Black piece goods discharged with Benzidine colours are often mercerised.

No. 15.

Aniline Black discharged with
Brilliant Geranine B. Benzo **Purpurine 4 B.**
Chrysophenine
(Chrysophenine
(Benzo Sky Blue
and afterwards mercerised.

No. 16.

Aniline Black discharged with
Heliotrope B B
(Benzo Sky Blue
(Chloramine Yellow
and afterwards mercerised.

Discharge Printing on Basic Dyestuffs.

The Benzidine dyestuffs are sometimes used for coloured discharges on basic dyestuffs dischargeable with oxidising agents.

No. 17.

Padded with:

    1 % tannic acid
    2 % tartar emetic.

Dyed with:

    0.7 % **Turquoise Blue B B.**

    Washed, dried, and printed with:

Orange **Discharge.**

Boil:
3 oz. or 30 grms. **Chloramine Orange G**
1¼ pints „ 250 „ water
¼ pint „ 100 „ mucilage of tragacanth
(1 : 100)
7 oz. „ 70 „ wheat starch; when cold add
1¼ pints „ 150 „ White Discharge I
¼ pint „ 100 „ albumen water 2 : 1
1000 grms.

Steam for ½ hour without pressure, wash and dry.

White Discharge I.

Boil:
14½ pints or 100 grms. chlorate of soda 76° Tw.
1 ⅔ lbs. „ 140 „ China clay
1 ⅔ galls. „ 120 „ water
8 lbs. „ 130 „ British gum; when luke warm add
1¼ lbs. „ 20 „ red prussiate of potash
2½ lbs. „ 40 „ citric acid dissolved in
1 ⅓ pints „ 100 „ water

For colour discharging of Alizarines with chloride of lime, Benzidine dyestuffs which resist the action of chlorine can be used.

No. 19.

Dyed with Alizarine and printed as follows:

Yellow Discharge.

Dissolve:
15 oz. or 150 grms. powdered tartaric acid and
1¼ lbs. „ 200 „ powdered citric acid in
1 pint „ 200 „ water, and add slowly
1¾ oz. „ 150 „ British gum and
3 oz. „ 50 „ **Chloramine Yellow** and
1¼ pints „ 250 „ water, then boil.
1000 grms.

No. 18.

Padded with:

    2 % tannic acid
    1 % tartar emetic.

Dyed with:

    1 % **New Victoria Blue B**
    2 % alum.

    Washed, dried and printed with:

Yellow Discharge.

Boil:
3 oz. or 30 grms. Chrysophenine
1¼ pints „ 250 „ water
½ pint „ 100 „ mucilage of tragacanth 1 : 100
7 oz. „ 70 „ wheat starch, and then add
1¼ pints „ 150 „ White Discharge I.
see No. 17.
¼ pint „ 100 „ albumen water 2 : 1
1000 grms.

Steam ½ hour without pressure, wash and dry.

No. 20.

The Benzidine dyestuffs are also suitable for adding to the resist to produce coloured resist effects under basic colours.

Yellow Resist.

Boil:
4½ oz. or 18 grms. Chloramine **Yellow**
dissolved in
1¼ pints „ 150 „ water, with
1½ pints „ 150 „ sulphite cellulose paste 60° Tw.
4¾ lbs. „ 250 „ British gum
1000 grms.

Cover Print Blue.

Dissolve in 50 grms. Acetine Blue
2¼ pints „ 250 „ acetine and add tragacanth thickening
1¼ pints „ 150 „ solution of tannic acid
1000 grms.

Print first with yellow resist, cover print with blue, as above, steam for one hour without pressure, wash, soap for 10 mins. cold, wash and dry.

Cotton Printing.
discharge printing on Aniline Black, basic dyestuffs etc.

Tafel 17

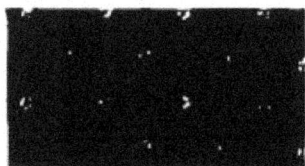

Aniline Black discharged with
Geranine G.

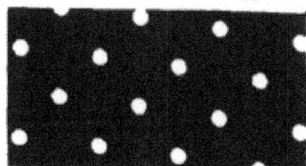

Aniline Black discharged with
Chloramine Yellow.

Aniline Black discharged with
Benzo Sky Blue.

Aniline Black discharged with
Benzo Purpurine 4 B.

Aniline Black discharged with Brilliant
Geranine B, Benzo Purpurine 4 B,
Chrysophenine; Benzo Sky Blue and
Chrysophenine Olive and afterwards
mercerised.

Aniline Black discharged with
Heliotrope B B, Benzo Sky Blue and
Chloramine Yellow, and afterwards
mercerised.

Turquoise Blue B B
discharged with Chloramine Orange G.

New Victoria Blue B
discharged with Chrysophenine.

Chloramine Yellow
discharged on Alizarine.

Chloramine Yellow
resist under Acetine Blue.

FARBENFABRIKEN vorm. FRIEDR. BAYER & Co., ELBERFELD

Table 17.

Discharge Printing on Basic Dyestuffs.

The following **basic dyestuffs** dyed on a tannic acid mordant, can be discharged with **oxidising agents** (chlorates, ferricyanide of potassium etc.)

Red Dyestuffs:
Rhodamine B.

Yellow Dyestuffs:
Auramine II.

Green Dyestuffs:
Brilliant Green
Emerald Green
Imperial Green G I
Methyl Green
Turquoise Blue G and B B.

Blue Dyestuffs:
New Victoria Blue B
Victoria Blue B.

Violet Dyestuffs:
Methyl Violet I B.

Brown Dyestuffs:
Bismarck Brown M, F F, L L. extra, R, F, R extra (fairly good).

Table 18.

No. 1.

E. Jantsch of the Cotton Manufacturing Co., Hilden, published some time ago a pamphlet treating of the practical application of discharge printing:

This firm dissolve substantive dyestuffs not affected by alkalies in an alkaline β-Naphtol solution, impregnate the cotton with this, print on a white or colour discharge (which serves both as a discharge and resist) cover print with a diazotised ice colour, steam for a short time, wash and soap. An example of this process of printing will perhaps demonstrate this more clearly:

Slop-pad flannelette with the following:

β-Naphtol solution.

16½ oz. or	420 grms.	β-Naphtol
3¼ noggs. „	740 „	caustic soda 36° Tw.
5 pints „	4000 cc.	water
1¼ pints „	1000 grms.	Turkey red oil
3 oz. „	120 „	**Benzo Sky Blue** dissolved in
17½ pints „	14000 „	water.

Instead of Benzo Sky Blue, Geranine G, Congo Orange G, Benzo Olive etc. can be used When dried the material is printed with the following:

Yellow Discharge and Resist.

2½ galls. or	500 grms.	White Discharge II see page 25
¼ gall. „	50 „	Extract of Persian berries 52° Tw.
3 lbs. 2 oz. „	50 „	citric acid powder
15 oz. „	15 „	tin crystals.

and afterwards cover printed with the following:

Ice Bordeaux.

18 oz. or	72 grms.	hydrochloride of x-Naphtyla- mine in paste 45%
1½ pints „	117 „	water
1½ noggs. „	36 „	hydrochloric acid 36° Tw.
30 oz. „	120 „	ice, then add slowly
2⅗ oz. „	11,4 „	nitrite dissolved in
1½ noggs. „	30 „	water, then filter and thicken with
6¼ pints „	615	British gum water 600:1000, and finally add
9½ oz. „	37,5 „	acetate of soda.

After cover printing steam for 5 mins. without pressure, wash, if necessary soap slightly in open state, wash and dry.

No. 2.

Pluszanski recently published an interesting article on conversion effects on dyed Benzidine grounds, of which the following is an example:

Dye which $2°$ **Brilliant Benzo Blue 6 B**, dry, print with White Discharge, cover print with Aniline Black containing Rhodamine 6 G, steam for $2-5$ mins. without pressure, wash and dry.

White Discharge.

2¼ pints or	23 grms.	mucilage of tragacanth (65:1000)
2½ lbs. „	29 „	tartaric acid powder
2 pints „	20 „	water
1 lb. „	9 „	carbonate of potash
2¼ noggs. „	13 „	caustic soda 96° Tw.
3½ pints „	34 „	mucilage of tragacanth (65:1000)
3 lbs. „	24 „	tin crystals
1½ lbs. „	12 „	soda
2½ lbs. „	20 „	acetate of soda
½ pint „	5 „	oil of turpentine.

Aniline Black Cover Print.

3 pints or 70 grms.	Aniline Black thickening
2 oz. „	24 „	**Rhodamine 6 G**
1½ noggs. „	7 „	glycerine 48° Tw.
{ ½ pint „	10 „	Aniline oil
{ 1½ noggs. „	10 „	hydrochloric acid 27° Tw.

Aniline Black Thickening.

11 oz. or	22 grms.	wheat starch
3½ lbs. „	110 „	British gum
2½ pints „	254 „	water
4½ oz. „	9 „	chlorate of soda
2½ pints „	230 „	water
4½ oz. „	9	yellow prussiate of potash.

If green or yellow conversion effects are desired when working with Aniline Black cover, then add to the black print colour in place of Rhodamine 6 G, Brilliant Green or Auramine II.

Cotton Printing.
(Discharges with tin.)

Table 1

1

Padded with: Beta-Naphtol, Benzo Sky Blue; Persian Berries
as a discharge and resist; cover printed with diazotised
Alpha-Naphtylamine.

2

Dyed with: Brilliant Benzo Blue 6 B;
Printed with: tin crystals discharge;
cover printed with: Aniline Black with Rhodamine 6 G.

(Discharges with oxidising agents.)

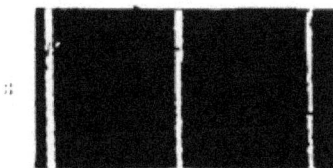

3

Dyed with: 4 , Benzo Blue B X;
Discharged with: chromate of lead.

4

Dyed with: 8 , Diazo Black B H N (Developer H);
Discharged with: chromate of lead and Pigment Red.

5

Dyed with: 2 , Brilliant Benzo Blue 6 B;
Discharged with: Pigment Red.

FARBENFABRIKEN vorm. FRIEDR. BAYER & Co. ELBERFELD

Table IX

Although the Benzidine Dyestuffs are mostly discharged with reducing agents, a large number of them, according to Smirnoff & Rosenthal can be discharged with oxidising agents. **The following Benzidine Dyestuffs are discharged by** oxidising **agents:**

Red Dyestuffs:

Benzo Purpurine 4 B, 10 B
Brilliant Congo G (good)
*Brilliant Geranine B, 3 B (good)
Brilliant Purpurine R (good)
Congo
Delta Purpurine 5 B (good)
*Geranine G, B B (good)
Rose Azurine G (good).

Orange Dyestuffs:

Benzo Orange R (yellow)
Congo Orange G (yellow)
Congo Orange R (yellow)
Toluylene Orange G.

Yellow Dyestuffs:

Thiazole Yellow.

Green Dyestuffs:

Benzo Dark Green
Benzo Green G, B B
Benzo Olive.

Blue Dyestuffs:

Benzo Azurine G (good)
Benzo Azurine 3 G (good)
Benzo Black Blue G, R, 5 G
Benzo Blue 2 B, 3 B, B X, RW
Benzo Chrome Black Blue B
Benzo Cyanine B (good)
Benzo Cyanine 3 B, R
Benzo Indigo Blue
Benzo Navy Blue
Benzo Sky Blue
Brilliant Azurine B (good)
Brilliant Azurine 5 G
Brilliant Azurine 5 G (coppered)
Brilliant Benzo Blue 6 B
Brilliant Benzo Blue 6 B (coppered)
Chicago Blue B, R
Diazo Black 3 B
Diazo Black R, R extra (undiazotised).
Diazo Blue (β-Naphtol) (yellowish)
Diazo Blue Black (brownish)

Violet Dyestuffs:

Azo Violet
Azo Violet (coppered)
Benzo Violet R
Heliotrope B B.

Brown Dyestuffs:

Benzo Black Brown (yellowish)
Benzo Brown B, B R, B X, G, G G, N B,
Benzo Brown N B X, R extra
Benzo Brown 5 R (yellow)
Benzo Chrome Brown B (brown)
Benzo Chrome Brown B (coppered) (brown)
Benzo Chrome Brown G
Benzo Chrome Brown G (oppered) (brown)
Benzo Chrome Brown R (brownish)
Benzo Chrome Brown R (coppered) (brown-
Benzo Dark Brown (yellowish)   (ish)
Congo Corinth G (good)
Diazo Brown G (brown)
Diazo Brown G (β-Naphtol) (brown)
Diazo Brown R extra (diazotised, Soda)
Direct Bronze Brown (yellow)
Direct Fast Brown B
Katigen Black Brown
Mikado Brown B (yellow)
Toluylene Brown B (good)
Toluylene Brown B B O (good)
Toluylene Brown M (good)
Toluylene Brown R.

Grey Dyestuffs:

Benzo Fast Grey (middling)
Benzo Fast Black (good)
Benzo Grey S extra
Diazo Blue Black (β-Naphtol)
Direct Blue Black B
Direct Deep Black T
Pluto Black B, G, R.

Black Dyestuffs (all brownish)

Diazo Black 3 B (β-Naphtol)
Diazo Black B H N (Developer H) (fairly good)
Diazo Black R (β-Naphtol)
Diazo Black R extra (Developers A & H)
Diazo Blue Black (β-Naphtol)
Diazo Brilliant Black R, B (β-Naphtol)
Direct Blue Black B (Paranitraniline)
Direct Blue Black B, N
Direct Deep Black T
Pluto Black B, G, R.

* These can be used with weak oxidising agents for colour discharging other dyestuffs whereas they are themselves discharged by strong oxidising agents.

Table 18.

No. 3.

Dyed with: 4 % **Benzo Blue B X.**
Discharged with: Yellow Discharge I.

Yellow Discharge I.

5½ lbs. or 450 grms. **chromate of lead in paste**
(Siegle)
2½ pints – 300 „ white discharge
2½ pints – 250 „ albumen water 2 : 1
1000 grms.

Boil:

White Discharge.

7¼ pints or 400 grms. chlorate of soda 76° Tw.
6 lbs. „ 190 „ China clay
3 pints „ 120 „ water
4 lbs. „ 130 „ British gum, and when
luke warm add
10 oz. „ 20 „ red prussiate of potash
1¼ lbs. „ 40 „ citric acid powder
2½ pints „ 100 „ water
1000 grms.

No. 4.

Dyed with: 8 % **Diazo Black B H N.**
Diazotised with: 4 lbs. nitrite
5½ pints hydrochloric acid 30° Tw.
200 galls. water
Developed with: 4 lbs. Developer II.
Discharged with: Yellow Discharge II and
Red Discharge.

Red Discharge.

5½ lbs. or 450 grms. **Rouge vif. E. N.**
Fabrique chemique de
Thann & de Mulhouse
2½ pints „ 300 „ White Discharge (as above)
2½ pints „ 250 „ Albumen water 2 : 1
1000 grms.

Yellow Discharge II.

5½ lbs. or 450 grms. **chromate of lead in paste**
(Siegle)
3¼ pints „ 450 „ White Discharge (please
refer to No. 1)
1 pint „ 100 „ Albumen water 2 : 1
1000 grms.

Steam for ¼ hour without pressure.

No. 5.

Dyed with: 2 % **Brilliant Benzo Blue 6 B.**
Discharged with: Red Discharge as given in No. 4.

Mercerising.

The following Benzidine Dyestuffs are suitable for mercerising purposes:

Red Dyestuffs:

Benzo Purpurine 10 B, 4 B
Brilliant Congo G
Brilliant Geranine B, 3 B
Brilliant Purpurine R
Congo Rubine
Delta Purpurine 5 B
Geranine G.

Orange Dyestuffs:

Benzo Orange R
Chloramine Orange G
Congo Orange G
Mikado Orange
Toluylene Orange G

Yellow Dystuffs:

Chloramine Yellow
Chrysophenine
Direct Yellow R
Mikado Yellow G
Thiazole Yellow.
Yellow P R superfine

Blue Dyestuffs:

Benzo Black Blue G, 5 G
Benzo Chrome Black Blue B
Benzo Cyanine B, 3 B, R
Benzo Sky Blue
Brilliant Benzo Blue 6 B.

Violet Dyestuffs:

Azo Violet.

Brown Dyestuffs:

Benzo Brown B
Benzo Chrome Brown B, G, R
Chloramine Brown G
Congo Corinth G
Toluylene Brown B, M, R

Grey Dystuffs:

Benzo Grey S extra
Diazo Black B H N
Direct Blue Black B
Direct Deep Black T.

Table 15

Cotton Printing.
(Mercerised Effects.)

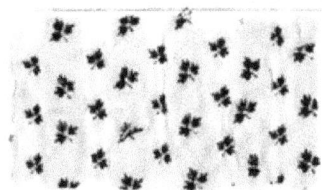

1

Chloramine Yellow on Aniline Black.

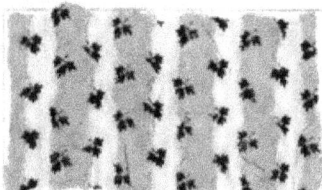

2

Geranine G on Aniline Black.

3

Brilliant Benzo Blue 6 B.

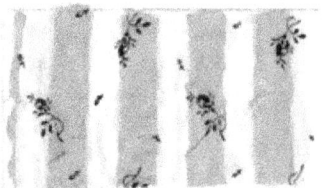

4

Thiazola Yellow and Brilliant Benzo
Blue 6 B on Aniline Black.

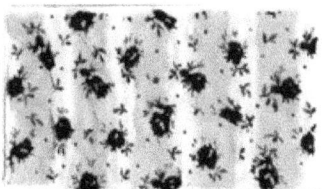

5

Congo Orange G on Aniline Black.

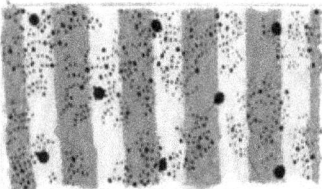

6

Azo Violet on Aniline Black.

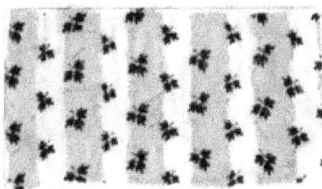

7

Brilliant Benzo Blue 6 B on
Aniline Black.

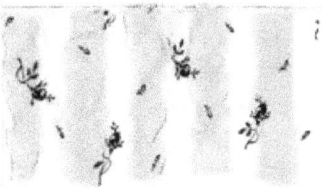

8

Brilliant Purpurine R on
Aniline Black.

9

Geranine G.

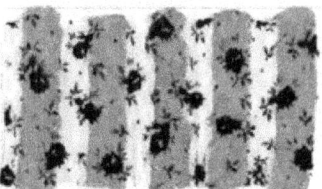

10

Direct Deep Black T.

FARBENFABRIKEN vorm. FRIEDR. BAYER & Co., ELBERFELD,

Table 19

The Benzidine Dyestuffs are extremely suitable for **mercerising** purposes, especially those unaffected by alkalies, or such as are temporarily altered but whose shade returns when washed.

The Benzidine Dyestuffs can be printed, as in patterns 1, 2, 4, 8 and 10 in stripe patterns, the colour being dissolved in water and thickened with gum water, then dried, steamed for ¼–½ hour without pressure, then run through caustic soda 32° Tw., washed and dried; or as in Nos. 3 and 9 with any thickening desired, then dried, steamed and cover printed in stripes with gum water, and run through caustic soda.

Directions for Printing.

¾–1 oz. or 5–7.5 grms. **Benzidine colour** dissolved in
½ pint „ 75 „ water, thickened with
1 gallon „ 1500 „ gum water 1 : 1.

Should the Benzidine colours not dissolve in the quality of water given, the solution is warmed up again with gum water; it is advisable to use only a good quality gum.

No. 1.
¾ oz. or 5 grms. **Chloramine Yellow.**

No. 2.
1 oz. or 7.5 grms. **Geranine G.**

No. 3.
1 oz. or 7.5 grms. **Brilliant Benzo Blue 6 B.**

No. 4.
1½ oz. or 0.25 grms. **Thiazole Yellow**
½ oz. or 3.75 grms. **Brilliant Benzo Blue 6 B**
(1½ pints or 100 grms. water.)

No. 5.
1 oz. or 7.5 grms. **Congo Orange G.**

No. 6.
1 oz. or 7.5 grms. **Azo Violet**
(2¼ pints „ 200 „ water).

No. 7.
1 oz. or 7.5 grms. **Brilliant Benzo Blue 6 B.**

No. 8.
1 oz. or 7.5 grms. **Brilliant Purpurine R.**

No. 9.
1 oz. or 7.5 grms. **Geranine G.**

No. 10.
1 oz. or 7.5 grms. **Direct Deep Black T.**

Printing on of thickened Caustic Soda.

As is well-known the Benzidine Dyestuffs dye and exhaust better on mercerised than on ordinary cotton. If pieces are printed with caustic soda, and then dyed with substantive colours, the printed part, which is mercerised, is dyed much darker. **Two-coloured** effects are thus obtained by means of one dyestuff and one roller. These goods can naturally be discharged white or in colours, if dischargeable dyes have been employed; they can further be diazotised and developed, treated according to requirement with sulphate of copper, bichromate of potash, or diazotised paranitraniline, or topped with basic colours etc. etc.

Directions.

Print the cotton with:

1 gallon or 1 litre caustic soda 106° Tw. thickened with
$^1\!/_4$ gallon „ 600 grms. gum water 1 : 1.

Then dry, wash and dye as given on page 22 with Benzidine dyestuffs.

No. 1.

Dyed with:

1.5 °/₀ **Brilliant Benzo Blue 6 B.**

Discharged with:

White Discharge II see page 25.

No. 2.

Dyed with:

2 °/₀ **Benzo Brown N B.**

No. 3.

Dyed with:

5 °/₀ **Direct Deep Black T.**

No. 4.

Dyed with:

2 °/₀ **Benzo Violet R.**

Discharged with:

0.5 °/₀ **Brilliant Green**
2.5 °/₀ **Auramine G**
25 °/₀ acetate of tin 2˚ Tw.
7.5 °/₀ tannic acid
2 °/₀ citric acid.

No. 5.

Dyed with:

2 °/₀ **Benzo Chrome Brown G**
and after-treated for ¹/₄ hour
with 3 °/₀ sulphate of copper and
2 °/₀ bichromate of potash.

No. 6.

Dyed with:

1 °/₀ **Brilliant Geranine B.**

No. 7.

Dyed with:

3 % **Benzo Purpurine 4 B.**

Discharged with:

9 % Extract of Persian berries 52° Tw.

9.8 % tin crystals

24.4 % acetate of tin 28° Tw.

2.4 % citric acid.

No. 8.

Dyed with:

3 % **Benzo Nitrol Brown G**
developed with diazotised Paranitraniline.

No. 9.

Dyed with:

1 % **Benzo Fast Black.**

Discharged with:

3 % **Rhodamine 6 G**

25 % acetate of tin 28° Tw.

7.5 % tannic acid

2 % citric acid.

No. 10.

Dyed with:

3 % **Congo Orange G.**

The white discharge patterns were steamed for 5 mins. without pressure and then washed.

The colour discharge patterns printed with basic colours were steamed for 10 mins. without pressure, and were then run through a lukewarm tartar emetic bath and afterwards washed; the Persian Berry Yellow Discharge pattern was steamed for 10 mins. without pressure and afterwards washed.

(Printed with thickened caustic soda.)

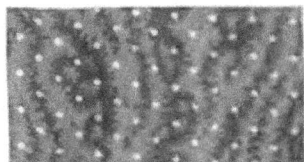

Dyed with: 15 Brilliant Benzo Blue 6 B
discharged with acetate of Cu.

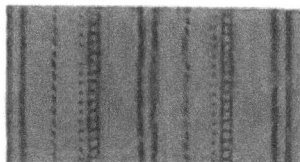

Dyed with: 2 Benzo Brown N B.

Dyed with: 5 Direct Deep Black T.

Dyed with: 2 Benzo Violet R;
discharged with: Brilliant Green and
Auramine G.

Dyed with: 2 Benzo Chrome Brown G.
coppered and chromed.

Dyed with: 1 Brilliant Geranine R.

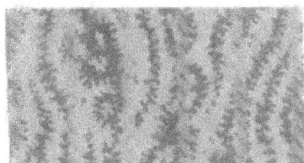

Dyed with: 3 Benzo Purpurine 4 B.
discharged with Persian Berry Yellow.

Dyed with: 4 Benzo Nitrol Brown G.
developed with diazotised
Paranitraniline.

Dyed with: 1 Benzo Fast Black;
discharged with: 3 Rhodamine 6 G.

Dyed with: 4 Congo Orange G.

FARBENFABRIKEN vorm. FRIEDR. BAYER & Co., ELBERFELD.

Zinc White **Printing.**

Goods first dyed with Benzidine dyestuffs and afterwards printed can be employed in some cases for printing with zinc white, viscose, tungstate of soda, then run through chloride of barium solution (Opaline effects,) etc.

Nos. 1—4 were printed with zinc white as follows:

No. 1.

Dyed with:
    1 % **Benzo Sky Blue.**

Printed with:
    zinc white.

No. 2.

Dyed with:
    0,5 % **Brilliant Geranine** B.

Printed with:
    zinc white.

No. 3.

Dyed with:
    5 % **Benzo Purpurine 4 B.**

Printed with:
    zinc white.

No. 4.

Dyed with:
    6 % **Benzo Chrome Black Blue B.**

Printed with:
    zinc white.

Zinc **White** Recipe.

7 lbs. or 120 grms.		zinc white	
½ pint	„	50	glycerine 28° Tw.
½ gallon	„	333	„ egg albumen water 1 : 1
3½ moggs.	„	67	„ water
3½	„	„	75	„ olive oil
2½	„	„	50	„ oil of turpentine.
		1025 grms.	

Steam for ½ hour without pressure.

Nos. 5—10.

Benzidine dyestuffs printed with zinc white, viscose, etc.

Cotton Printing.

(Printed with zinc white, viscose, etc.)

Dyed with: 1 Benzo Sky Blue;
Printed with: zinc white.

Dyed with: 0·5 Brilliant Geranine B;
Printed with: zinc white.

Dyed with: 5 Benzo Purpurine 4 B;
Printed with: zinc white.

Dyed with: 6 Benzo Chrome Black
Blue B; Printed with: zinc white.

Benzo Sky Blue.

Heliotrope B B.

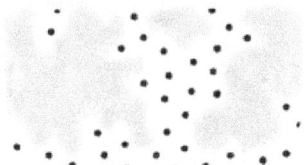

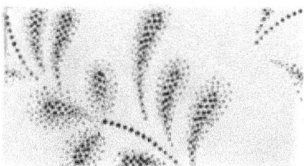

Chloramine Yellow.

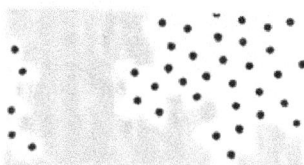

Benzo Sky Blue.

Heliotrope B B.

Chloramine Yellow (shaded).

Linings.

Cotton linings are often padded on the **slop padding** machine instead of dyeing in a beck or jig.

Slopped and dry:

No. 1.

1 oz. or 22 grms.	**Benzo** Chrome Brown **B**
1 oz. „ 55 „	**Benzo Chrome Brown G**
¹⁄₄ oz. „ 1 „	**Chloramine Yellow**
9 oz. „ 50 „	phosphate of soda
25 galls. „ 22 litres	water.

No. 2.

1½ oz. or 6 grms.	**Chloramine Yellow**
1½ oz. „ 6 „	**Benzo Chrome Brown B**
1½ oz. „ 25 „	**Benzo Chrome Brown G**
12 oz. „ 50 „	phosphate of soda
39 galls. „ 22 litres	water.

No. 3.

¹⁄₄ oz. or 72 grms.	**Direct** Deep Black **G**
¹⁄₄ oz. „ 24 „	Benzo Chrome Brown **G**
5 oz. „ 50 „	phosphate of soda
13½ galls. „ litres	water.

No. 4.

¹⁄₄ oz. or 3 grms.	Chloramine Yellow
¹⁄₄ oz. „ 2 „	**Benzo** Chrome Brown **B**
6 oz. „ 50 „	phosphate of soda
19½ galls. „ 22 litres	water.

No. 5.

1 oz. or 10 grms.	**Chloramine Yellow**
¹⁄₄ oz. „ 5 „	**Benzo Chrome Brown G**
5 oz. „ 50 „	phosphate of soda
13½ galls. „ 22 litres	water.

No. 6.

¹⁄₄ oz. or 6 grms.	**Chloramine Yellow**
¹⁄₄ oz. „ 6 „	**Benzo** Chrome **Brown B**
¹⁄₄ oz. „ 15 „	**Benzo** Chrome Brown **G**
¹⁄₄ oz. „ „	**Direct** Deep Black **G**
4 oz. „ 50 „	phosphate of soda
11½ galls. „ 22 litres	water.

No. 7.

10 oz. or 10 grms.	**Chloramine Yellow**
15 oz. „ 60 „	**Benzo Chrome Brown B**
5 oz. „ 20 „	**Benzo** Chrome Brown **G**
3 oz. „ 12 „	**Direct Deep Black G**
6 oz. „ 24 „	phosphate of soda
31½ galls. „ 20 litres	water.

Indigo padded with:

No. 1.

2 lbs. or 1 kilo	**Chloramine Yellow**
3½ oz. „ 100 grms	phosphate of soda
20 galls. „ 100 litres	water.

No. 2.

4 lbs. or 2 k'los	**Brilliant Geranine B**
3½ oz. „ 100 grms.	common salt
20 galls. „ 100 litres	water.

Cotton Printing.

(Stop-padded linings).

Benzo Chrome Brown R, Benzo Chrome
Brown G, Chloramine Yellow.

Chloramine Yellow, Benzo Chrome
Brown R, Benzo Chrome Brown G.

Direct Deep Black G,
Benzo Chrome Brown G.

Chloramine Yellow.
Benzo Chrome Brown G.

Chloramine Yellow,
Benzo Chrome Brown G.

Chloramine Yellow, Benzo Chrome
Brown R, Benzo Chrome Brown G,
Direct Deep Black G.

Chloramine Yellow, Direct Deep Black G,
Benzo Chrome Brown R,
Benzo Chrome Brown G.

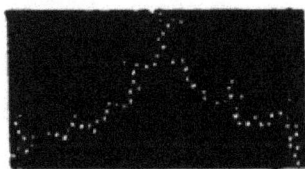

Discharged Indigo padded with
Chloramine Yellow.

Discharged Indigo padded with
Brilliant Geranine R.

FARBENFABRIKEN vorm. FRIEDR. BAYER & Co. ELBERFELD.

The following **Benzidine** dyestuffs are unaffected by acid (when tested with acetic acid).

Red Dyestuffs:

Benzo Purpurine 4 B (slightly affected)
Brilliant Congo (scarcely affected)
Brilliant Geranine B, 3 B
Delta Purpurine 5 B, 7 B (slightly affected)
Geranine G, B B
Red PR
Rose Azurine B, G (slightly affected)

Orange Dyestuffs:

Chloramine Orange G (scarcely affected)
Congo Orange R, G
Mikado Orange
Toluylene Orange G

Yellow Dyestuffs:

Chloramine Yellow
Chrysamine
Chrysophenine
Direct Yellow R
Mikado Yellow
Yellow PR

Green Dyestuffs:

Benzo Green B B, G,
Benzo Olive (scarcely affected)

Blue Dyestuffs:

Benzo Azurine G, 3 G
Benzo Blue R W, B X, 2 B, 3 B
Benzo Chrome Black Blue B
Benzo Cyanine B, 3 B, R
Benzo Indigo Blue
Benzo Navy Blue B
Benzo Sky Blue
Benzo Black Blue G, 5 G, R
Brilliant Azurine B, 5 G
Brilliant Benzo Blue 6 B
Diazo Blue, 3 R (β-Naphtol)
Diazo Blue Black
Diazo Indigo Blue (β-Naphtol) (scarcely affected)
Diazo Black B, R, R extra

Violet Dyestuffs:

Azo Violet (coppered)
Benzo Violet R
Diazo Violet (β-Naphtol)
Heliotrope B B

Brown Dyestuffs:

Benzo Brown B, B R, B X
Benzo Nitol Brown G, 2 R (Paranitraniline)
Benzo Black Brown
Chloramine Brown G
Diazo Brown G
Diazo Brown G (β-Naphtol)
Mikado Brown B
Toluylene Brown B

Grey Dyestuffs:

Benzo Fast Grey (scarcely affected)
Benzo Fast Black
Diazo Blue Black (β-Naphtol)
Direct Blue Black B
Direct Deep Black T
Pluto Black B, R, G

Black Dyestuffs:

Benzo Chrome Black X
Diazo Black 3 B (β-Naphtol) R extra (developer A & H)
Direct Blue Black B, X
Direct Deep Black G, R, T, R W, E, E extra
Pluto Black B, G, R.

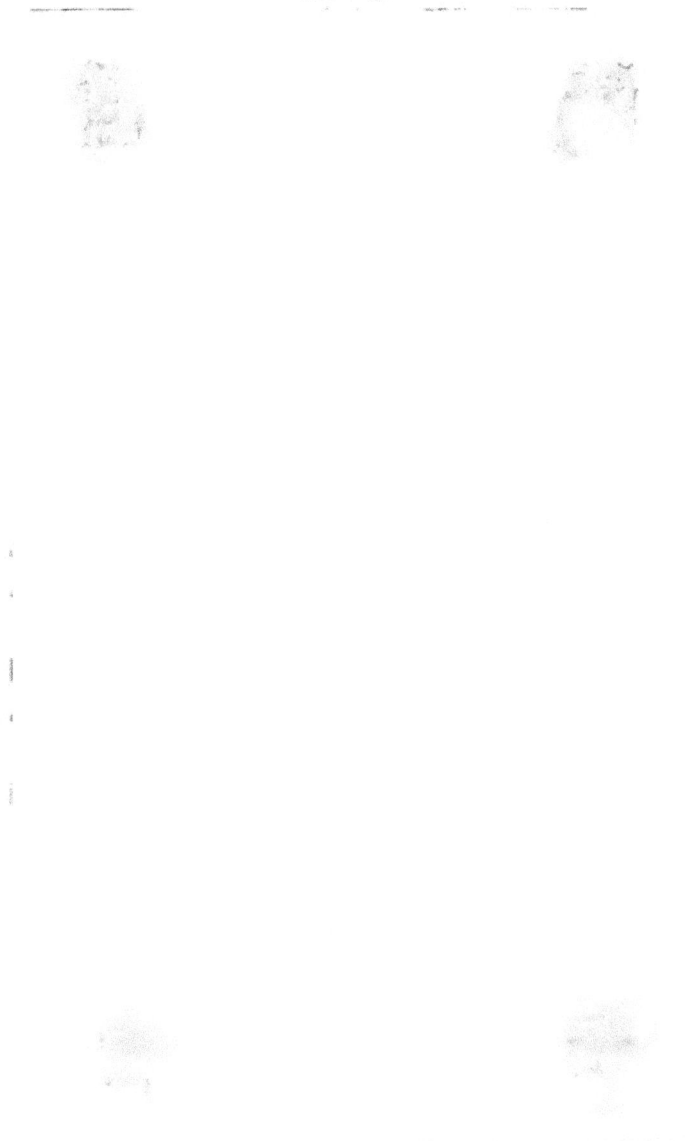

Dyed with: Alizarine Red S X X 20 ; finished with: Chrysamine G.

The following **Benzidine dyestuffs** are unaffected by alkalies (when spotted with ammonia etc.):

Red Dyestuffs:

Benzo Purpurine 1 B, 4 B, 6 B, 10 B
Brilliant Congo G, R
Brilliant Geranine B, 3 B
Brilliant Purpurine R
Congo Red
Delta Purpurine 5 B
Geranine G
Red P R
Rose Azurine G.

Orange Dyestuffs:

Chloramine Orange G
Congo Orange G, R
Mikado Orange G
Toluylene Orange G.

Yellow Dyestuffs:

Chloramine Yellow
Chrysophenine
Direct Yellow R
Mikado Yellow G
Yellow P R.

Green Dyestuffs:

Benzo Green G, B B.

Blue Dyestuffs:

Benzo Blue G N, 2 B, 3 B, R W
Benzo Chrome Black Blue B
Benzo Cyanine B, 2 B, 3 B, R
Benzo Indigo Blue
Benzo Navy Blue B
Benzo Sky Blue
Benzo Black Blue G, 5 G, R
Brilliant Benzo Blue 6 B
Chicago Blue B, R
Diazo Blue Black
Diazo Dark Blue 3 B (β-Naphtol)
Diazo Black B, R, R extra.

Violet Dyestuffs:

Diazo Violet (β-Naphtol)
Heliotrope.

Brown Dyestuffs:

Benzo Brown B, G, 5 R
Benzo Chrome Brown R
Benzo Nitrol Brown G (Paranitraniline)
Benzo Black Brown
Chloramine Brown G
Congo Corinth G
Congo Rubine
Diazo Brown G
Diazo Brown R extra (diazotised and
    developed with soda)
Direct Bronce Brown
Direct Fast Brown B, G G
Mikado Brown B
Toluylene Brown B, B B O, M, R.

Grey Dyestuffs:

Benzo Fast Black
Pluto Black G.

Black Dyestuffs:

Benzo Fast Black
Benzo Black S extra
Diazo Blue Black (β-Naphtol)
Diazo Brilliant Black (β-Naphtol)
Diazo Black B, R, R extra, 3 B, B H N
    (β-Naphtol)
Direct Blue Black B, N
Direct Deep Black G, R, T, E, E extra
Pluto Black B, G, R.

Printed with Steam Colours; finished with Chrysamine G.

FARBENFABRIKEN vorm. FRIEDR. BAYER & Co., ELBERFELD.

77

The following **Benzidine Dyestuffs** are unchanged when ironed.

Red Dyestuffs:

Benzo Purpurine 4B
Geranine G, BB
Red PR.

Orange Dyestuffs:

Chloramine Orange G
Congo Orange R, G
Mikado Orange G
Toluylene Orange G.

Yellow Dyestuffs:

Chloramine Yellow
Chrysophenine.

Green Dyestuffs:

Benzo Olive.

Blue Dyestuffs:

Benzo Blue 3 B, R W
Benzo Chrome Black Blue B
Benzo Cyanine B, 3 B, R
Benzo Indigo Blue
Benzo Sky Blue
Benzo Black Blue 5 G
Brilliant Azurine 5 G
Brilliant Benzo Blue 6 B
Chicago Blue B, R
Diazo Blue Black
Diazo Dark Blue 3 B (β-Naphtol)
Diazo Indigo Blue (β-Naphtol)
Diazo Black B, R, R extra.

Brown Dyestuffs:

Benzo Brown B, BR, BX, G, GG, R extra, 5 R
Benzo Nitrol Brown (Paranitraniline)
Benzo Black Brown
Chloramine Brown G
Diazo Brown G
Diazo Brown G (β-Naphtol) Paranitraniline)
Mikado Brown B.

Grey Dyestuffs:

Benzo Fast Grey
Benzo Fast Black.

Black Dyestuffs:

Benzo Chrome Black X
Benzo Fast Black
Diazo Blue Black (β-Naphtol)
Diazo Indigo Black (β-Naphtol)
Diazo Black B, 3 B, B H N, R, R extra
(β-Naphtol)
Direct Blue Black B, X
Direct Deep Black T, E
Pluto Black B, G, R.

The following **Benzidine Dyestuffs** are fast to **chlorine**:

Red Dyestuffs:

Brilliant Geranine B, 3 B (middling)
Geranine G, B B (middling)

Orange Dyestuffs:

Chloramine Orange G
Congo Orange G, R (to a certain extent)
Mikado Orange G.

Yellow Dyestuffs:

Chloramine Yellow
Chrysophenine
Direct Yellow R
Mikado Yellow G.

Brown Dyestuffs:

Chloramine Brown G.

Of the **Benzidine Dyestuffs** the following are the **fastest to light**:

Red Dyestuffs:

Brilliant Geranine B, 3 B
Geranine G, B R.

Orange Dyestuffs:

Chloramine Orange G
Mikado Orange.

Yellow Dyestuffs:

Chloramine Yellow
Chrysamine
Chrysophenine
Mikado Yellow.

Green Dyestuffs:

Benzo Olive.

Blue Dyestuffs:

Benzo Azurine G, 3 G, R (coppered)
Benzo Blue KW (coppered)
Benzo Chrome Black Blue B
Benzo Indigo Blue
Benzo Black Blue G, 5 G, R
Benzo Navy Blue B
Brilliant Azurine 5 G (coppered)
Brilliant Benzo Blue 6 B (coppered).

Brown Dyestuffs:

Benzo Chrome Brown (chromed and coppered)
Chloramine Brown G.

Grey Dyestuffs:

Benzo Fast Black.

Of the **Benzidine Dyestuffs** the following are suitable for **cotton yarn printing**:

Red Dyestuffs:

Benzo Purpurine 4 B
Geranine G.

Orange Dyestuffs:

Benzo Orange R.

Yellow Dyestuffs:

Chloramine Yellow.

Blue Dyestuffs:

Benzo Blue
Benzo Sky Blue.

Direct Yarn Printing.

	No. 1.		No. 2.	
Boil:	**Blue.**	Boil:	**Red.**	

Boil:
6 oz. or 50 grms. **Benzo Sky Blue**
5¼ lbs. „ 500 „ British gum and
6⅜ pints „ 670 „ water
1000 grms.

Boil:
4 oz. or 50 grms. **Geranine G**
5¼ lbs. „ 500 „ British gum and
6⅜ pints „ 670 „ water
1000 grms.

Steam for 1 hour without pressure.

Discharge Printing With Tin On Yarn.

The Benzidine colours when dyed on cotton yarn can be discharged white or coloured with tin in exactly the same way as when dyed on piece goods. (See page 24—37.)

Tin Crystals Discharge.

Boil:
5¼ pints or 424 grms. water
½ lb. „ 50 „ wheat starch
3¼ pints „ 300 „ acetate of tin 32° Tw.
1¾ pints „ 180 „ gum water 1:1
5 oz. „ 50 „ tin crystals and when cold
add
7¼ oz. „ 20 „ citric acid
1000 grms.

Steam for 2—5 mins. without pressure, wash and dry.

Cotton Yarn Printing.
(Direct Printing.)

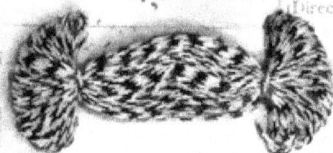

Printed with: 3% Benzo Sky Blue.

Printed with: 2% Geranine G.

(Discharge Printing with tin.)

Dyed with: 3% Congo Orange G;
discharged with: tin crystals discharge.

Dyed with: 4% Benzo Purpurine 4 B;
discharged with: tin crystals discharge.

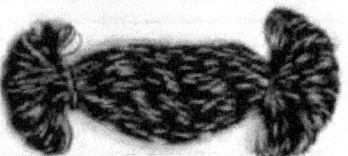

Dyed with: 3% Benzo Violet R;
discharged with: tin crystals discharge.

Dyed with: 1% Benzo Fast Black;
discharged with: tin crystals discharge.

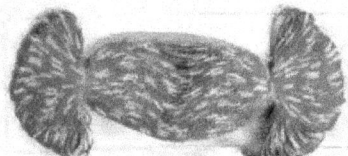

Dyed with: 1% Geranine;
discharged with: tin crystals discharge.

Colour Discharge Printing With Tin.

No. 1.

Dyed with: 6% Benzo **Chrome Black Blue B**
Discharged with: 4% **Auramine G**
method same as in No. 6.

No. 2.

Dyed with: 3% Benzo **Chrome Brown G**
Discharged with: 1% **Methyl Violet 6 B**
method same as in No. 6.

No. 3.

Dyed with: 4% **Benzo Blue B X**
Discharged with: 3% **Rhodamine 6 G**.

No. 4.

Dyed with: 2% Brilliant Benzo **Blue 6** B
Discharged with: 3% Auramine **II**.

Red Discharge.

	6 oz. or	30 grms.	**Rhodamine 6 G**
	3 pints „	200 „	water
	2½ pints „	300 „	acetic acid 9° Tw. (30%)
	1 pint „	100 „	mucilage of tragacanth
			65 : 1000
	3½ noggs. „	100 „	acetate of tin 32° Tw.
	1½ pints „	180 „	acetic acid tannic acid
			solution 1 : 1
		1000 grms.	

Yellow Discharge.

	6 oz. or	30 grms.	**Auramine II**
	3 pints „	200 „	water
	2½ pints „	300 „	acetic acid 9° Tw. (30%)
	1 pint „	100 „	mucilage of tragacanth
			65 : 1000
	3½ noggs. „	100 „	acetate of tin 32° Tw.
	1½ pints „	180 „	acetic acid tannic acid
			solution 1 : 1
		1000 grms.	

No. 5.

Dyed with: 8% **Pluto Black B**
Discharged with: 4% **Auramine G**
method same as in No. 6.

No. 6.

Dyed with: 3% Benzo Chrome Brown B
Discharged with: 0.5% Brilliant **Green crystals**
2.5% Auramine **G.**

Green Discharge.

	1 oz. or	5 grms.	Brilliant **Green crystals**
	5 oz. „	25 „	Auramine **G**
	2½ pints „	280 „	water
	2½ pints „	300 „	acetic acid 9° Tw. (30%)
	1 pint „	100 „	mucilage of tragacanth
			65 : 1000
	3½ noggs. „	100 „	acetate of tin 32° Tw.
	2 oz. „	10 „	tin crystals
	1½ pints „	180 „	acetic acid tannic acid
			solution 1 : 1
		1000 grms.	

Steam for 2 minutes without pressure, run through a cold bath of tartar emetic, wash and dry.

Table 36.

Cotton Yarn Printing.

(Colour discharges with tin.)

Dyed with: 6% Benzo Chrome Black Blue B;
Discharged with: 4% Auramine G.

Dyed with: 3% Benzo Chrome Brown G;
Discharged with: 1% Methyl-Violet 6 B.

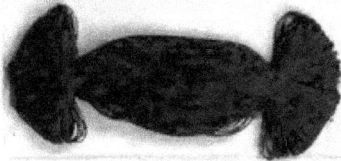

Dyed with: 4% Benzo Blue BX;
Discharged with: 3% Rhodamine 6 G.

Dyed with: 2% Brilliant Benzo Blue 6 B;
Discharged with: 3% Auramine II.

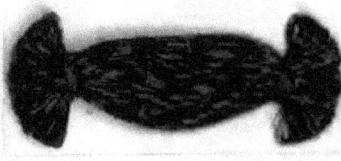

Dyed with: 8% Pinto Black B;
Discharged with: 4% Auramine G.

Dyed with: 3% Benzo Chrome Brown B;
Discharged with: ½% Brilliant Green
crystals and 2% Auramine G.

(Printing with caustic soda and afterwards dyeing).

Printed with: Caustic Soda;
Dyed with: 2% Benzo Green G.

Printed with: Caustic Soda;
Dyed with: 2% Brilliant Benzo Blue 6 B.

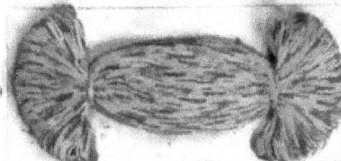

Printed with: Caustic Soda;
Dyed with: 3% Benzo Purpurine 4 B.

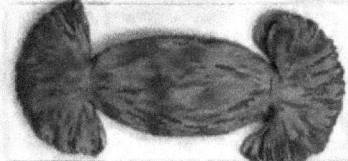

Printed with: Caustic Soda;
Dyed with: 2% Brilliant Geranine B.

FARBENFABRIKEN vorm. FRIEDR. BAYER & Co. ELBERFELD.

Printing Caustic Soda on Cotton Yarn.

By printing caustic soda on cotton yarn and then dyeing with Benzidine Colours similar effects as on cotton pieces (see page 63) are obtained since the mercerised cotton dyes darker than the part not printed.

Print with:

8½ pints or 1000 grms. Caustic soda 106·4° Tw. thickened with

1 pint „ 100 „ gum water 1 : 1.

dry, wash in running water and dye as mentioned on page 63.

No. 7.

2 Benzo Green G.

No. 8.

2% Brilliant Benzo Blue 6 B.

No. 9.

3% Benzo Purpurine 4 B

No. 10.

2% Brilliant Geranine B.

Wool Printing.

The following Benzidine Colours can be printed on wool stuffs and yarns:

Red Dyestuffs:

Benzo Purpurine 4 B
Brilliant Geranine B, 3 B
Delta Purpurine 5 B
Geranine G
Rose Azurine B.

Orange Dyestuffs:

Benzo Orange R
Congo Orange G

Yellow Dyestuffs:

Chloramine Yellow
Chrysophenine.

Blue Dyestuffs:

Benzo Azurine G
Benzo Blue 2 B. 3 B
Benzo Sky Blue.

Brown Dyestuffs:

Heliotrope B B (Bordeaux).

Table 27.

Wool Stuff Printing.

The Benzidine Dyestuffs are also adapted for printing chlormated wool stuffs.

No. 1.

Bod:

  4 oz. or 20 grms. **Geranine** G

  3¼ lbs. „ 1500 „ British gum

  6¼ pints „ 600 „ water, and then add

  4 oz. „ 20 „ phosphate of potash

  [2040 grms.]

No. 2.

4 oz. or 20 grms. **Benzo Orange** R

  the other components same as in No. 1

No. 3.

4 oz. or 20 grms. Benzo Sky **Blue**

  the other components same as in No. 1.

No. 4.

4 oz. or 20 grms. **Benzo** Purpurine 4 B

  the other components same as in No. 1.

Steam for 1 hour without pressure, wash and dry

Table 27.

Wool Printing.
(Wool stuff.)

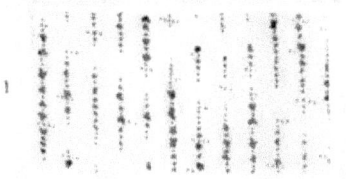

1. Wool printed with: 2%, Geranine G.

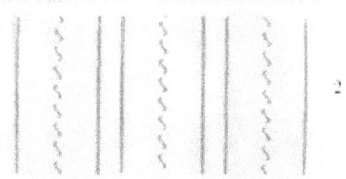

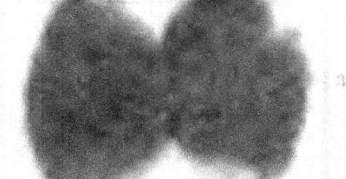

2. Wool printed with: 2%, Benzo Orange R.

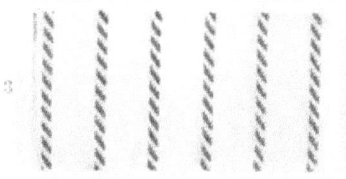

3. Wool printed with: 2%, Benzo Sky Blue.

4. Wool printed with: 2%, Benzo Purpurine 4 B.

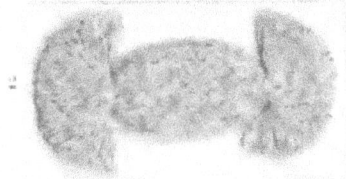

(Wool Yarn Printing.)   (Slubbing Printing.)

1. Printed with: 3%, Congo Orange G.   Benzo Purpurine

2. Printed with: 3%, Chrysophenine.   Chrysophenine

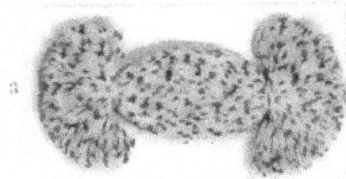

3. Printed with: 3%, Geranine G.   Benzo Sulphon Azurine R.

FARBENFABRIKEN vorm. FRIEDR. BAYER & Co., ELBERFELD.

Wool Yarn Printing.

Print the colour on chlorinated wool yarn, steam moist for 1 hour without pressure, wash and dry.

No. 1

1 oz. or 30 grms.	Congo **Orange G**
1½ gallon „ 200 „	water
7½ pints „ 750 „	flour thickening
1 noggin „ 20 „	acetic acid 9° Tw
1000 grms.	

No. 2.

6 oz. or ? grms.	Chrysophenine
1½ gallon „ 200 „	water
7½ pints „ 750 „	flour thickening
1 noggin „ 20 „	acetic acid 9° Tw
1000 grms.	

No. 3.

6 oz. or 30 grms.	Geranine **G**
1½ gallon „ 200 „	water
7½ pints „ 750 „	flour thickening
1 noggin „ 20 „	acetic acid 9° Tw
1000 grms.	

Flour Thickening.

10 lbs. or 100 grms. flour	
5½ gallons „ 900 „ water.	

Slubbing Printing.

The Benzidine Dye-stuffs have found considerable application in slubbing printing.

No. 1.

Boil: **Benzo Purpurine 4 B.**

10 oz. or 50 grms.	Benzo **Purpurine 4 B**
3½ lbs. „ 300 „	British gum
6½ pints „ 650 „	water
1000 grms.	

No. 2.

Boil: Chrysophenine.

6 oz. or 30 grms.	Chrysophenine
3½ lbs. „ 300 „	British gum and
6½ pints „ 670 „	water
1000 grms.	

No. 3.

Boil: **Brilliant Sulphon Azurine R.**

6 oz. or 30 grms.	Brilliant **Sulphon** Azurine **R** in paste
6 lbs. „ 300 „	British gum and
3½ pints „ 350 „	water, and then add
1 pint „ 100 „	solution of ammonia
1000 grms.	

The following **Benzidine Dyestuffs** are adapted for **slubbing printing:**

Red Dyestuffs:

Benzo Purpurine 4 B
Brilliant Congo R
Brilliant Geranine B
Delta Purparine 5 B
Geranine G, B B.

Yellow Dyestuffs:

Chloramine Yellow
Chrysophenine
Curcumine W, S.

Green Dyestuffs:

Benzo Green G.

Blue Dyestuffs:

Brilliant Sulphon Azurine R
Sulphon Azurine D.

Brown Dyestuffs:

Chloramine Brown G.

No. 4.

Boil: Brilliant Geranine B.

6 oz. or 30 grms. Brilliant Geranine B
3¾ lbs. „ 300 „ British gum and
4¾ pints „ 470 „ water and add
¾ pint „ 70 „ acetic acid 9° Tw. (30%)
{ 6 oz. „ 30 „ chrome alum dissolved in
{ 1 pint „ 100 „ water
1000 grms.

No. 5.

Boil: Benzo Green G.

1½ oz. or 50 grms. Benzo Green G
3 lbs. 2 oz. „ 250 „ British gum and
6 pints „ 600 „ water, and add
1 pint „ 100 „ acetate of ammonia
1000 grms.

No. 6.

Boil: Chloramine Brown G.

8 oz. or 40 grms. Chloramine Brown G
3¾ lbs. „ 300 „ British gum and
5¾ pints „ 590 „ water, then add
¾ pint „ 70 „ acetic acid 9° Tw. (30%)
1000 grms.

No. 7.

Boil: Chloramine Yellow.

8 oz. or 40 grms. Chloramine Yellow
3¾ lbs. „ 300 „ British gum and
6 pints „ 600 „ water, then add
½ pint „ 60 „ acetic acid 9° Tw. (30%)
1000 grms.

No. 8.

Boil: Brilliant Congo R.

10 oz. or 50 grms. Brilliant Congo R
3¾ lbs. „ 300 „ British gum and
6½ pints „ 650 „ water
1000 grms.

No. 9.

Boil: Sulphon Azurine D.

10 oz. or 50 grms. Sulphon Azurine D
3¾ lbs. „ 300 „ British gum and
5½ pints „ 550 „ water, and then add
1 pint „ 100 „ acetate of ammonia
1000 grms.

No. 10.

Boil: Curcumine S.

12 oz. or 60 grms. Curcumine S
3¾ lbs. „ 300 „ British gum and
5¾ pints „ 580 „ water, then add
½ pint „ 60 „ acetic acid 9° Tw. (30%)
1000 grms.

No. 11.

Boil: Geranine G.

6 oz. or 30 grms. Geranine G
3¾ lbs. „ 300 „ British gum and
4¾ pints „ 470 „ water, then add
¾ pint „ 70 „ acetic acid 9° Tw. (30%)
and when cold add
{ 6 oz. „ 30 „ chrome alum dissolved in
{ 1 pint „ 100 „ water
1000 grms.

No. 12.

Boil: Congo Orange G.

6 oz. or 30 grms. Congo Orange G
3¾ lbs. „ 300 „ British gum and
6 pints „ 600 „ water, then add
¾ pint „ 70 „ acetic acid 9° Tw. (30%)
1000 grms.

No. 13.

Boil: Curcumine W.

8 oz. or 40 grms. Curcumine W
3¾ lbs. „ 300 „ British gum and
6 pints „ 600 „ water, then add
½ pint „ 60 „ acetic acid 9° Tw. (30%)
1000 grms.

After printing the goods are steamed for 1 hour without pressure, washed and dried.

Table 28

Wool Printing.
(Slubbing Printing.)

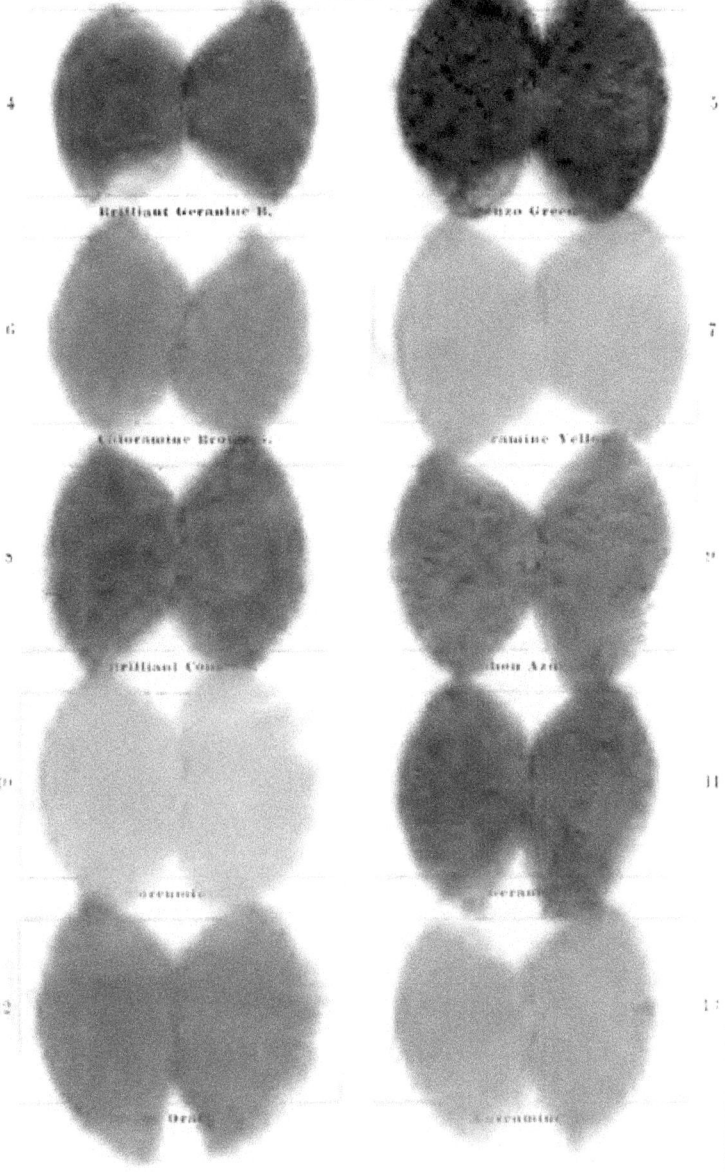

4

Brilliant Geranine B.

5

Benzo Green

6

Chloramine Brown

7

Chloramine Yellow

8

Brilliant Congo

9

Chamois Azo

10

Cerumaic

11

Geranine

12

Orange

13

Cerumaine

FARBENFABRIKEN vorm. FRIEDR. BAYER & Co., ELBERFELD.

Half Wool Printing.

(Wool and cotton.)

The following Benzidine Dyestuffs are adapted for **printing half** wool:

Red Dyestuffs:
Benzo Purpurine 4 B
Brilliant Geranine B.

Orange Dyestuffs:
Congo Orange G.

Yellow Dyestuffs:
Chrysophenine.

Blue Dyestuffs:
Benzo Sky Blue.

Brown Dyestuffs:
Toluylene Brown.

No. 1.		No. 2.
Boil:		Boil:
1 oz. or 20 grms. **Brilliant Geranine B**		The same as No. 1 but with
5 lbs. „ 500 „ British gum and		1 oz. or 20 grms. Congo Orange G.
6½ pints „ 600 „ water, and then add		
1 oz. „ 20 „ borax		
1000 grms.		

Steam for 1 hour without pressure, wash and dry.

Half Wool Printing.

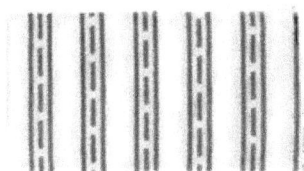

2 Brilliant Geranine B.

2 Congo Orange G.

Half Wool Dyeing.

(Discharge Printing.)

Wool and mercerised Cotton.

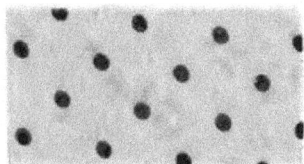

Dyed with: 0·4 Congo Orange R;
Discharged with: 2 Rhodaline Violet.

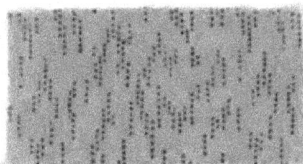

Dyed with: 0·45 Geranine G;
Discharged with:
1·5 New Methylene Blue 3 R.

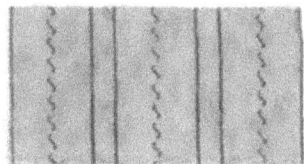

Dyed with: 0·4 Brilliant Benzo Blue
6 B and 0·04 Alkali Blue 6 B;
Discharged with: 1 Rhodamine 6 G.

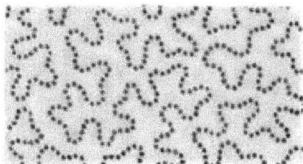

Dyed with: 0·4 Chrysophenine;
Discharged with: 4 Rhodaline Violet.

Halfwool dyed with:
6 Direct Deep Black G,
1 Sulphon Cyanine G B extra,
Sulphon Blue Black;
Discharged with: 6 Rhodamine 6 G
and 0·8 Auramine II.

Halfwool dyed with:
2 Benzo Chrome Brown B,
0·4 Benzo Chrome Brown G;
Discharged with:
1·5 Brilliant Green crystals and
1·5 Auramine G.

Half Wool Dyeing.

The **Benzidine Colours** are very suitable for the **dyeing of half wool**, and if dischargeable Benzidine Dyestuffs be used useful discharge effects can be obtained.

The affinity of the Benzidine dyestuffs to both fibres is indicated in a general way in the following tables, but it is to be noted that the temperature of the dye bath, volume of water etc. are important factors in dyeing.

1. The following colours dye **cotton and wool equally** (or almost equally) i. e. in similar shade and strength:

> Benzo Purpurine 4 B, 10 B. Congo Red. Hessian Purple X. — Benzo Orange R. Congo Orange R. Orange T.A. Toluylene Orange G. Thiazol Yellow. — Benzo Green G. — Benzo Azurine G, 3G. Benzo Blue 2 B, 3 B, B X, RW. Benzo Cyanine B. Chicago Blue B. Diazo Blue Black. Diazo Black B, R. Benzo Brown N B X. Benzo Chrome Brown B, G, R, 3 R. Benzo Dark Brown. Benzo Black Brown. Congo Corinth G. Direct Fast Brown B. Toluylene Brown R, M, B. Direct Blue Black B, X. Direct Deep Black G. R. Pluto Black G.

2. The following colours dye the **wool darker**, but in the same or almost the same shade as the cotton:

> Brilliant Geranine 3 B. Delta Purpurine 5 B. Geranine G. Hessian Purple B. Chrysamine G, R. Chrysophenine. Benzo Dark Green. — Diazo Red Blue. Brilliant Benzo Blue 6 B. — Congo Rubine.

3. The following colours dye the cotton darker but in the same or almost the same shade as the wool:

> Chloramine Orange. Chloramine Yellow. Curcumine S. Direct Yellow R. Mikado Yellow. Brilliant Azurine B. Benzo Chrome Black Blue B. Peazo Sky Blue. Chicago Blue R. Diazo Black B H X.

4. The following colours dye the **cotton** and the **wool very different** shades:

> Benzo Olive. Benzo Black Blue G, R. Benzo Brown N B R.

5. The following colours are adapted for shading the wool, as they dye well in a neutral bath:

> Cochineal Scarlet P S. Croceine Scarlet 3 B. Brilliant Croceine 3 B. Orange G T. Indian Yellow G. — Acid Green 3 B. — New Victoria Blue B. Lazuline Blue R. Sulphon Cyanine. — Alkali Violet R. Acid Violet H W. Sulphon Black. Sulphon Blue Black.

Table 29.

Half Wool Discharge Printing.

The Benzidine dyestuffs are of considerable importance for half wool dyeing.

No. 3.

Dyed with:

0·1 % **Congo Orange R**
20 % Glauber's salt.

Discharged with:

4 oz. or	20 grms.	**Rhoduline Violet**
14 oz. „	70 „	wheat starch
½ gallon „	220 „	gum water 1 : 1
½ gallon „	200 „	water
2½ pints „	250 „	acetic acid 9° Tw. (30 %)
½ pint „	100 „	acetate of tin 32° Tw.
⎰ 12 oz. „	60 „	tannic acid dissolved in
⎱ 2½ noggs. „	60 „	acetic acid 9° Tw. (30 %)
4 oz. „	20 „	citric acid
	1000 grms.	

No. 4.

Dyed with:

0·15 % **Geranine G**
20 % Glauber's salt.

Discharged with:

3 oz. or	15 grms.	**New Methylene Blue 3 R**
14 oz. „	70 „	wheat starch
½ gallon „	220 „	gum water 1 : 1
2½ pints „	255 „	water
½ gallon „	260 „	acetic acid 9° Tw. (30 %)
½ pint „	100 „	acetate of tin 32° Tw.
⎰ 12 oz. „	60 „	tannic acid dissolved in
⎱ 2½ noggs. „	60 „	acetic acid 9° Tw. (30 %)
4 oz. „	20 „	citric acid
	1000 grms.	

No. 5.

Dyed with:

0·1 % **Brilliant Benzo Blue 6 B**
0·03 % **Alkali Blue 6 B**
20 % Glauber's salt.

Discharged with:

8 oz. or	40 grms.	**Rhodamine 6 G**
14 oz. „	70 „	wheat starch
½ gallon „	220 „	gum water 1 : 1
2½ pints „	250 „	water
1¼ pints „	130 „	acetic acid 9° Tw. (30 %)
1½ pints „	150 „	acetate of tin 32° Tw.
⎰ 12 oz. „	60 „	tannic acid dissolved in
⎱ 2½ noggs. „	60 „	acetic acid 9° Tw. (30 %)
4 oz. „	20 „	citric acid
	1000 grms.	

No. 6.

Dyed with:

0·1 % **Chrysophenine**
30 % Glauber's salt.

Discharged with:

6 oz. or	30 grms.	**Rhoduline Violet**
14 oz. „	70 „	wheat starch
½ gallon „	220 „	gum water 1 : 1
1 pint „	160 „	water
2½ pints „	260 „	acetic acid 9° Tw. (30 %)
1½ pints „	150 „	acetate of tin 32° Tw.
⎰ 15 oz. „	75 „	tannic acid dissolved in
⎱ 3 noggs. „	75 „	acetic acid 9° Tw. (30 %)
4 oz. „	20 „	citric acid
	1000 grms.	

No. 7.	No. 8.

No. 7.

Dyed with:

6 °/₀ **Direct Deep Black G**

1 °/₀ **Sulphon Cyanine G R extra**

¹⁄₄ °/₀ **Sulphon Blue Black**

20 °/₀ Glauber's salt.

Boil for ¹⁄₂ hour, and let the goods run for another ¹⁄₂ hour without steam.

Boil: Discharged with:

12 oz. or 60 grms. **Rhodamine 6 G**

1¹⁄₂ oz. „   8   „ **Auramine II**

14 oz. „ 70   „ wheat starch

¹⁄₂ gallon „ 22   „ acetic acid 9° Tw. (30 °/₀)

1¹⁄₂ pint „ 150   „ gum water 1 : 1

2¹⁄₂ pints „ 250   „ acetate of tin 32° Tw.
                and then add

1¹⁄₂ lbs. „ 100   „ tin crystals

{ 2 lbs. „ 160   „ tannic acid dissolved in

{ 1¹⁄₂ pints „ 100   „ acetic acid 9° Tw. (30 °/₀)

4 oz. „ 20   „ citric acid

        1000 grms.

Steam for ¹⁄₂ hour without pressure.

No. 8.

Dyed with:

2 Benzo **Chrome Brown B**

4 Benzo **Chrome Brown G**

10 °/₀ Glauber's salt crystals

Enter at 125° Faht. bring slowly to the boil, shut off steam and then run the goods for ¹⁄₂ hour longer.

                Discharged with:

3 oz. or 15 grms. Brilliant Green (crystals)

3 „ 15   „ **Auramine G**

14 oz. „ 70   „ wheat starch

¹⁄₂ pint „ 100   „ acetic acid Tw. (30 °/₀)

¹⁄₂ pint „ 90   „ water

1¹⁄₂ pints „ 190   „ gum water 1 : 1

2¹⁄₂ pints „ 250   „ acetate of tin 32° Tw.

1¹⁄₂ lbs. „ 100   „ tin crystals

1¹⁄₂ pints „ 150   „ solution of tannic acid 1 : 1

4 oz. „ 20   „ citric acid

        1000 grms.

After printing with discharges the pieces are steamed for ¹⁄₂—1 hour without pressure, according to the depth of the engraving and quantity of tin crystals used, and then run through a cold bath of tartar emetic, washed and dried.

9

Dyed with: 1 Benzo Purpurine 4B;
Discharged with: 1 Auramine G.

10

Dyed with: 4 Benzo Cyanine B;
Discharged with: 1 Auramine G.

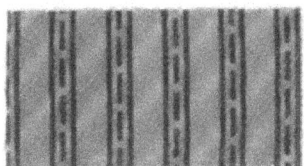

11

Dyed with: 4 Chrysophenine and
1.5 Brilliant Green;
Discharged with: 1.5 Auramine G.

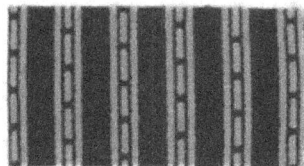

12

Dyed with: 1 Geranine G;
Discharged with: 1 Auramine G.

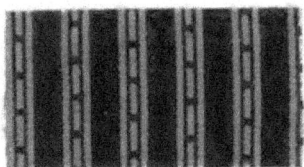

13

Dyed with: 4 Benzo Chrome Brown B;
Discharged with: 1 Auramine G.

14

Dyed with: 4 Direct Fast Brown M;
Discharged with: 1 Auramine G.

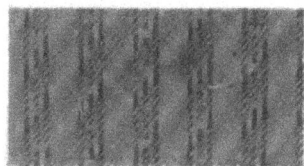

15

Dyed with: 1 Benzo Orange R;
Discharged with: 1.5 Brilliant Green
and 1.5 Auramine G.

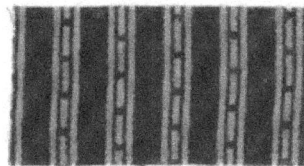

16

Dyed with: 1 Benzo Purpurine 10 B;
Discharged with: 1 Auramine G.

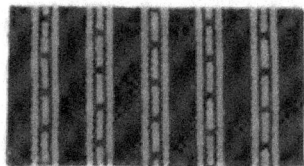

17

Dyed with: 4 Toluylene Brown M;
Discharged with: 4 Auramine G.

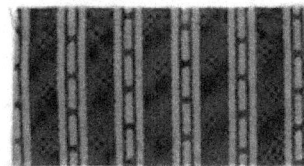

18

Dyed with: 1 Chicago Blue B;
Discharged with: 1 Auramine G.

FARBENFABRIKEN vorm. FRIEDR. BAYER & Co., ELBERFELD.

No. 9.	No. 10.
Dyed with: 1°₀ **Benzo Purpurine 4 B**	Dyed with: 4°₀ **Benzo Cyanine B**
10°₀ Glauber's salt.	10°₀ Glauber's salt.
Discharged with: 4°₀ **Auramine G.**	Discharged with: 4°₀ **Auramine G.**

No. 11.	No. 12.
Dyed with: 4°₀ **Chrysophenine**	Dyed with: 4°₀ **Geranine G**
10°₀ Glauber's salt.	10°₀ Glauber's salt.
Discharged with: { 1·5°₀ **Brilliant Green crystals** { 1·5°₀ **Auramine G.**	Discharged with: 4°₀ **Auramine G.**

No. 13.	No. 14.
Dyed with: 4°₀ **Benzo Chrome Brown R**	Dyed with: 4°₀ **Direct Fast Brown B**
10°₀ Glauber's salt.	10°₀ Glauber's salt.
Discharged with: 4°₀ **Auramine G.**	Discharged with: 4°₀ **Auramine G.**

No. 15.	No. 16.
Dyed with: 4°₀ **Benzo Orange R**	Dyed with: 4°₀ **Benzo Purpurine 10 B**
10°₀ Glauber's salt.	10°₀ Glauber's salt.
Discharged with: { 1·5°₀ **Brilliant Green crystals** { 1·5°₀ **Auramine G.**	Discharged with: 4°₀ **Auramine G.**

No. 17.	No. 18.
Dyed with: 4°₀ **Toluylene Brown M**	Dyed with: 4°₀ **Chicago Blue B**
10°₀ Glauber's salt.	10°₀ Glauber's salt.
Discharged with: 4°₀ **Auramine G.**	Discharged with: 4°₀ **Auramine G.**

In dyeing raise temperature to boil in ½ hour, boil for ½ hour, run ½ hour without steam, rinse and dry. Afterwards print with discharge colour, steam for ½ hour without pressure, and finally pass through a cold tartar emetic bath, wash and dry.

Yellow Discharge.

8 oz. or 40 grms.	**Auramine G**	
14 oz. „ 70 „	wheat starch	
1 pint „ 100 „	acetic acid 9° Tw. (30°₀)	
½ pint „ 70 „	water	
1½ pint „ 140 „	gum water 1 : 1	
2½ pints „ 250 „	acetate of tin 32° Tw.	
2 lbs. „ 100 „	tin crystals	
1½ pints „ 150 „	solution of tannic and acetic acid 1 : 1	
4 oz. „ 20 „	citric acid powder	
1000 grms.		

Green Discharge.

3 oz. or 15 grms.	Auramine G	
3 oz. „ 15 „	**Brilliant Green** crystals	
14 oz. „ 70 „	wheat starch	
1 pint „ 100 „	acetic acid 9° Tw. (30°₀)	
1½ pints „ 120 „	water	
1½ pints „ 140 „	gum water 1 : 1	
2½ pints „ 250 „	acetate of tin 32° Tw.	
1½ lbs. „ 120 „	tin crystals	
1½ pints „ 150 „	solution of tannic and acetic acid 1 : 1	
4 oz. „ 20 „	citric acid powder	
1000 grms.		

Silk Printing.

The following Benzidine Dyestuffs can be printed on **silk goods**:

Red Dyestuffs:

Benzo Purpurine 1 B
Brilliant Geranine B
Delta Purpurine 5 B
Rose Azarine B.

Orange Dyestuffs:

Benzo Orange R
Chloramine Orange G
Congo Orange G, R.

Yellow Dyestuffs:

Chloramine Yellow
Chrysophenine.

Blue Dyestuffs:

Benzo Azurine G
Benzo Sky Blue.

Violet Dyestuffs:

Heliotrope B B (red violet)

Brown Dyestuffs:

Congo Corinth G, B.

Grey Dyestuffs:

Benzo Fast Grey.

Table 30.

The Benzidine dyestuffs can also be used for direct printing on silk

No. 1.

Printed with:

Boil:

4 oz. or	20 grms.	**Heliotrope B B**
3½ lbs. „	300 „	British gum
6½ pints „	600	water, and then add
4 oz.	20 „	phosphate of soda
	1000 grms.	

No. 2.

Printed with:

Boil:

4 oz. or	20 grms.	**Brilliant Geranine B**
3½ lbs. „	300 „	British gum and
6½ pints „	600	water, and then add
4 oz. „	20 „	phosphate of soda
	1000 grms.	

Steam for 1 hour without pressure, wash and dry.

Silk Discharge Printing.

Dyed on silk the following Benzidine dyestuffs can be discharged with zinc powder:

Red Dyestuffs:
Benzo Purpurine 4 B, 4 B
Brilliant Geranine B
Geranine G
Rose Azurine G.

Orange Dyestuffs:
Benzo Orange R
Congo Orange G, R.

Yellow Dyestuffs:
Chrysamine G
Chrysophenine.

Green Dyestuffs:
Benzo Olive (yellow).

Blue Dyestuffs:
Benzo Blue 2 B, B X
Benzo Chrome Black Blue B
Benzo Cyanine B, R
Benzo Cyanine 3 B
Benzo Indigo Blue
Brilliant Azurine 5 G
Brilliant Benzo Blue 6 B
Brilliant Sulphon Azurine R
Diazo Blue β-Naphtol
Sulphon Azurine D (yellow).

Violet Dyestuffs:
Azo Violet
Heliotrope B B.

Brown Dyestuffs:
Congo Corinth B, G.

Grey Dyestuffs:
Benzo Grey S extra (yellow).

Black Dyestuffs:
Benzo Black S extra (yellow)
Diazo Blue Black B (yellowish)
Diazo Brilliant Black B (β-Naphtol)
Diazo Brilliant Black R (β-Naphtol)
Diazo Black R (β-Naphtol)
Direct Blue Black B (yellowish)

Table

No. 3.

Dyed with:
3 % Brilliant Benzo Blue 6 B
(boiled off liquor and acetic acid).

Discharged with:
zinc powder and bisulphite of soda as given
on page 42.

Steam for ½ hour without pressure, give a
slight sour, wash and dry.

No. 4.

Dyed with:
5 % Congo Corinth G
(boiled off liquor and acetic acid).

Discharged with:
Dissolve:

3 oz. or 6 grms. Methylene Blue B B
2½ pints „ 91 „ water add
6¼ pints „ 300 „ gum water 1:1; and
    when cold add
10 lbs. „ 820 „ zinc powder; then add
    slowly
5¼ pints „ 280 „ bisulphite of soda 60°
    1000 grms. [Tw.

After printing steam for ½ hour without
pressure, wash and dry.

95

Table 19

Silk Printing.
(Direct Printing.)

1

2

Printed with: 2   Heliotrope B B.   **Printed with: 2   Brilliant Geranine B.**

(Discharge Printing.)

3

4

Dyed with: Brilliant Benzo Blue 6 B;   **Dyed with: 5 Congo Corinth G;**
Discharged with: zinc powder.   **Discharged with: 0.6 Methylene**
                                           Blue B R and zinc powder.

(Yarn Printing.)

5

6

Printed with: 2   Benzo Orange R.   Printed with: 2   Brilliant Benzo Blue 6 B.

(Yarn Discharge Printing.)

7

8

Dyed with: 4   Geranine G; Discharged   **Dyed with: 4   Benzo Purpurine 4 B;**
with: 3   Fast Acid Violet 10 B.   **Discharged with: zinc powder.**

Half Silk Printing.
(Direct Printing.)

9

10

Printed with: 6   Benzo Orange R.   **Printed with: 6   Benzo Purpurine 4 B.**

FARBENFABRIKEN vorm. FRIEDR. BAYER & Co. ELBERFELD.

The following dyestuffs are **not destroyed by zinc powder,** and are therefore adapted for **colour discharging** Benzidine dyestuffs dyed on silk:

Red Dyestuffs:

Rhoduline Red B, G
Saffranine F F extra.

Yellow Dyestuffs:

Quinoline Yellow.

Blue Dyestuffs:

Induline B, 6 B
Methylene Blue B B.

Violet Dyestuffs:

Rhoduline Violet.

Silk Yarn Printing.

The following Benzidine Colours are adapted for printing silk yarn :

Red Dyestuffs:

Brilliant Geranine B.

Orange Dyestuffs:

Benzo Orange R.

Blue Dyestuffs:

Benzo Sky Blue
Brilliant Benzo Blue 6 B.

Brown or Bordeaux Dyestuffs:

Congo Corinth G.

Table 30.

No. 5.			No. 6.		
Orange.			**Blue.**		
4 oz or 20 grms.		Benzo Orange R dissolved in	4 oz. or 20 grms.		Brilliant Benzo Blue 6 B dissolved in
3½ pints	360	water, and thickened with	3½ pints	360	water, and thickened with
6 pints	600	mucilage of traga- canth 65 : 1000	6 pints	600	mucilage of traga- canth 65 : 1000
4 oz.	20	phosphate of soda	4 oz.	20	phosphate of soda
1000 grms.			1000 grms.		

Steam for 1 hour without pressure, wash and dry.

Discharge Printing on Silk Yarn.

Those Benzidine Dyestuffs which can be discharged with zinc powder (or tin crystals) after having been dyed on silk yarn, are the same as those given on page 96 for dyeing silk stuffs.

No. 7.

Dyed with:

1½ Geranine G.

Discharged with:

Blue Discharge.

Boil

6 oz.	30 grms.	**Fast Acid Violet 10 B**	
1½ pints	105	"	water
4½ pints	450	"	gum water 1:1
10 oz.	48	"	wheat starch
5 oz.	24	"	dextrine and
1 pint	100	"	water, and then add
1 pint	120	"	acetate of tin 32° Tw.
12 oz.	60	"	tin crystals
	1000 grms.		

No. 8.

Dyed with:

1 Benzo Purpurine 1 B.

Discharged with:

Zinc powder as same page 42.

Steam for ½ hour without pressure, wash and dry.

The following **undischargeable** dyestuffs are adapted for **colour discharges with tin** on silk yarn dyed with dischargeable Benzidine colours:

Red Dyestuffs:
Saffranine F F extra.

Yellow Dyestuffs:
Auramine II
Quinoline Yellow.

Green Dyestuffs:
Brilliant Green crystals
Fast Green bluish
Fast Green extra bluish
Fast Light Green
Acid Green G G, B B N, 3 B.

Blue Dyestuffs:
Fast Acid Blue B
Fast Acid Violet 10 B.

Violet Dyestuffs:
Methyl Violets
Acid Violets.

The following Benzidine Dyestuffs dyed on silk are fast to milling:

Red Dyestuffs:

Diazo Bordeaux (Developer A)
Rose Azurine G, B.
Yellow P R (Developer A)

Orange Dyestuffs:

Chloramine Orange G
Yellow P R (Developer F)

Yellow Dyestuffs:

Chloramine Yellow
Direct Yellow R.

Blue Dyestuffs:

Brilliant Azurine 5 G
Brilliant Sulphon Azurine R
Diazurine B (Developer A)
Diazo Blue (Developer A)
Diazo Red Blue 3 R (Developer A)
Sulphon Azurine D.

Violet Dyestuffs:

Heliotrope.

Brown Dyestuffs:

Chloramine Brown G.
Diazo Brilliant Black R, B (Developed with
                                    soda)
Diazo Brown G, V (Developer A)
Diazo Brown R extra (Developed with soda)
Diazo Brown R extra (Developer H)
Diazo Brown R extra (chromed and coppered).

Black Dyestuffs:

Benzo Fast Black (Developer A)
Diazo Brilliant Black R, B (Developer B)
Diazo Blue Black (Developer A)
Diazo Black R, G, H, B (Developer A)

The following Benzidine Dyestuffs dyed on silk are fast to alkali (ammonia):

Red Dyestuffs:

Benzo Purpurine 1 B, 4 B, 6 B, 10 B
Brilliant Congo R
Brilliant Geranine B, 3 B
Brilliant Purpurine R
Delta Purpurine 5 B
Diazo Bordeaux (Developer A)
Geranine B B
Hessian Purple N
Rose Azurine G, B
Yellow P R (Developer A).

Orange Dyestuffs:

Chloramine Orange G
Mikado Orange R
Toluylene Orange R.

Yellow Dyestuffs:

Chloramine Yellow
Chrysophenine
Direct Yellow R.

Blue Dyestuffs:

Benzo Black Blue G, R
Brilliant Sulphon Azurine R
Diazo Blue (Developer A)
Diazo Blue Black (undiazotised)
Diazo Red Blue 3 R (Developer A)
Sulphon Azurine D.

Violet Dyestuffs:

Benzo Violet R
Heliotrope
Heliotrope B B.

Brown Dyestuffs:

Benzo Brown G, G G, B, B X, R extra
Benzo Chrome Brown B, G, R
Chloramine Brown G
Congo Corinth G, B
Diazo Brown G, V (Developer A)
Diazo Brown R extra (developed with soda
Diazo Brown R extra (Developer H)
Diazo Brown R extra (chromed and coppered)
Toluylene Brown B, R

Black Dyestuffs:

Benzo Fast Black
Benzo Fast Black (Developer A)
Diazo Brilliant Black R, B (Developer B)
Diazo Blue Black (Developer A)
Diazo Black R, G, H, B (Developer A).

The following Benzidine Dyestuffs dyed on silk are fairly fast to water:

Red Dyestuffs:

Benzo Purpurine 1 B, 4 B
Brilliant Congo R
Diazo Bordeaux (Developer A)
Yellow P R (Developer A).

Orange Dyestuffs:

Benzo Orange R
Chloramine Orange G
Congo Orange
Mikado Orange R
Mikado Orange G
Yellow P R (Developer F).

Yellow Dyestuffs:

Chloramine Yellow
Chrysamine G
Chrysamine R
Chrysophenine.

Blue Dyestuffs:

Benzo Azurine G
Benzo Black Blue R, G
Diazo Blue (Developer A)
Diazo Red Blue 3 R (Developer A)
Diazurine B (Developer A)
Sulphon Azurine D.

Brown Dyestuffs:

Chloramine Brown G
Diazo Brown R extra (Developed with soda)
Diazo Brown R extra (Developer H)
Diazo Brown R extra (chromed and coppered)
Diazo Brown G, V (Developer A)
Diazo Brown V
Diazo Brilliant Black R, B (Developed with
soda)

Black Dyestuffs:

Benzo Fast Black Developer A)
Diazo Blue Black (Developer A)
Diazo Black R, G, H, B (Developer A)
Diazo Brilliant Black R, B (Developer B).

The following Benzidine Dyestuffs dyed on **silk** are **fast to acid** (acetic acid):

Red Dyestuffs:

Benzo Purpurine 4 B, 4 B
Brilliant Congo R
Brilliant Geranine B, 3 B
Brilliant Purpurine R
Delta Purpurine 5 B
Diazo Bordeaux (Developer A)
Geranine B B
Hessian Purple N
Rose Azurine G, B
Yellow P R (Developer A).

Orange Dyestuffs:

Congo Orange
Chloramine Orange G
Mikado Orange R, G
Toluylene Orange G
Yellow P R (Developer F).

Yellow Dyestuffs:

Chloramine Yellow
Chrysamine G, R
Chrysophenine.

Blue Dyestuffs:

Benzo Azurine G
Benzo Black Blue G, R
Brilliant Azurine 5 G
Brilliant Sulphon Azurine R
Diazo Blue (Developer A)
Diazo Blue Black (undiazotised)
Diazo Red Blue 3 R (Developer A)
Diazo B (Developer A)
Sulphon Azurine D.

Violet Dyestuffs:

Benzo Violet R
Heliotrope
Heliotrope B B

Brown Dyestuffs:

Benzo Brown G, G G, B, B X, R extra
Benzo Chrome Brown G, R
Chloramine Brown G
Diazo Brown G, V
Diazo Brown G, V (Developer A)
Diazo Brown R extra (Developer H)
Diazo Brown R extra (Developed with soda)
Diazo Brilliant Black R, B (Developed with
Toluylene Brown R, B.   (soda)

Black Dyestuffs:

Benzo Fast Black
Benzo Fast Black (Developer A)
Diazo Black R, G, H, B (Developer A)
Diazo Blue Black (Developer A).
Diazo Brilliant Black R, B (Developer A)

Table 10.

Half Silk Printing.

The Benzidine Colours are also employed in **half silk printing.** The following were printed with:

Boil:
No. 9.
12 oz. or 60 grms. **Benzo Orange R**
3 lbs. 2 oz. „ 250 „ British gum and
6½ pints „ 670 „ water, and then add
4 oz. „ 20 „ phosphate of soda
1000 grms.

No. 10.
The same as No. 9 but with
12 oz. or 60 grms. **Benzo Purpurine 1 B.**

Table 31.

No. 11.
The same as No. 9 but with
12 oz. or 60 grms. **Benzo Chrome Brown B.**

No. 12.
The same as No. 9 but with
12 oz. or 60 grms. **Delta Purpurine 5 B.**

Boil:
No. 13.
4 oz. or 20 grms. **Geranine G**
3½ lbs. „ 300 „ British gum and
6½ pints „ 600 „ water, and then add
4 oz. „ 20 „ phosphate of soda
1000 grms.

Boil:
No. 14.
2 oz. or 10 grms. **Brilliant Benzo Blue 6 B**
3½ lbs. „ 300 „ British gum and
6½ pints „ 670 „ water, and then add
4 oz. „ 20 „ phosphate of soda
1000 grms.

Steam for 1 hour without pressure, wash and dry.

Half Silk Dyeing.

The Benzidine dyestuffs are very suitable for **half silk dyeing**. In their behaviour to silk and cotton they vary considerably. Many of them dye the cotton and leave the silk undyed, whilst others dye both silk and cotton the same or different shades. Colours of the latter class dye the silk more than the cotton. They are dyed with the addition to the bath of Glauber's salt and soap.

1. The following colours dye **silk and cotton equally**:

Benzo Purpurine 4 B, Brilliant Congo R, Brilliant Geranine 3 B, Delta Purpurine 5 B, Geranine G, Rose Azurine B, G. Chrysamine G, R, Chrysophenine. Benzo Dark Green. Congo Corinth, Toluylene Brown B B O.

2. The following colours leave the **silk white or almost white** and dye the **cotton** only:

Chloramine Orange G. Direct Yellow R. — Benzo Sky Blue (soap), Benzo Black Blue G (soap), Benzo Blue 2 B, 3 B, Brilliant Benzo Blue 6 B, Benzo Chrome Black Blue B (almost white). Diamine Black R O.

3. The following colours dye the **silk less than the cotton** (or the cotton more than the silk):

Chloramine Yellow (slightly), Thiazole Yellow (almost the same). — Benzo Green G. Benzo Blue RW (slightly). Benzo Indigo Blue (slightly). Toluylene Brown R.

4. The following colours dye the **silk a different colour to the cotton**:

Azo Blue (silk redder), Benzo Azurine G (silk reddish, cotton a deeper blue). Azo Violet (silk redder, cotton darker). Benzo Brown B (silk redder), Benzo Chrome Brown B, G, R and 3 R (silk lighter shade, somewhat yellower than the cotton). Diamine Black B O (silk redder).

Half Silk Printing.

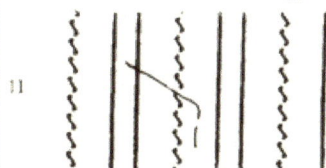

Half Silk printed with:
6   Benzo Chrome Brown B.

Half Silk printed with
6   Delta Purpurine 5 B.

Half Silk printed with:
2   Geranine G.

Half Silk printed with:
1   Brilliant Benzo Blue 6 B.

(Discharge Printing with zinc)

Congo Corinth G.

Toluylene Brown R R O.

Chrysophenine.

Delta Purpurine 5 B.

Brilliant Geranine 3 B.

Benzo Blue 2 R.

FARBENFABRIKEN vorm. FRIEDR. BAYER & Co., ELBERFELD.

107

Half Silk Discharge Printing.

The following Benzine dyestuffs dyed on half silk can be discharged with **zinc powder**:

Red Dyestuffs:

Benzo Purpurine 4 B
Brilliant Congo G and R
Brilliant Geranine B, 3 B
Geranine G
Rose Azurine G, R.

Orange Dyestuffs:

Benzo Orange R
Congo Orange R.

Yellow Dyestuffs:

Chrysamine G, R
Chrysophenine.

Green Dyestuffs:

Benzo Dark Green
Benzo Green G
Benzo Olive.

Blue Dyestuffs:

Azo Blue
Benzo Blue 2 B, 3 B, B X, R W
Benzo Azurine G
Benzo Cyanine 3 B
Benzo Indigo Blue
Benzo Sky Blue
Benzo Black Blue G
Brilliant Azurine 5 G
Brilliant Sulphon Azurine R
Brilliant Benzo Blue 6 B
Sulphon Azurine D.

Violet Dyestuffs:

Azo Violet
Heliotrope B B.

Brown Dyestuffs:

Benzo Brown B R, G G, B
Benzo Chrome Brown B, G, R, 3 R
Congo Corinth G
Heliotrope
Toluylene Brown B B O, R.

Black Dyestuffs:

Diamine Black R O, B O.

Table 31.

Discharge Printing With Zinc Powder.

Colours dyed with dischargeable Benzidine dyestuffs can be easily discharged with zinc powder and bisulphite.

White Discharge.

Mix:
12 lbs. or 333 grms. zinc powder, finely sifted
1 gallon „ 333 „ gum water 1 : 1, cool down with ice, and add gradually
7½ pints „ 334 „ bisulphite of soda 66° Tw.
1000 grms.

Print on with a brush furnisher, steam for ½—1 hour without pressure, give a weak soap, wash and dry.

No. 1.
4% Congo Corinth G
10% Glauber's salt
2% soap.
Dye for 1 hour at 195° Faht.

No. 2.
4% Toluylene Brown B B O
10% Glauber's salt
2% soap.

No. 3.
2% Chrysophenine
10% Glauber's salt
2% soap.

No. 4.
4% Delta Purpurine
10% Glauber's salt
2% soap.

No. 5.
2% Brilliant Geranine 3 B
10% Glauber's salt
4% soap.

No. 6.
3% Benzo Blue 2 B
10% Glauber's salt, and later add
1% acetic acid.

No. 7.

  Geranine G
  10% Glauber's salt
  4% soap.

No. 8.	**No. 9.**
4% **Benzo Blue RW**	4% **Benzo Brown B**
10% Glauber's salt	10% Glauber's salt
3% soap.	3% soap
No. 10.	**No. 11.**
4% **Benzo Green G**	4% **Rose Azurine B**
10% Glauber's salt.	10% Glauber's salt
4% soap.	3% soap.
No. 12.	**No. 13.**
3 **Benzo Sky Blue**	2% **New Toluylene Brown M**
10% Glauber's salt.	10% Glauber's salt
	2% soap.
No. 14.	**No. 15.**
1% **Congo Orange R**	2% **Chrysamine G**
10% Glauber's salt	10% Glauber's salt
2% soap.	3% soap.

Half Silk Printing.

Discharge Printing with ....

Geranine G.

Benzo Blue R W.

Benzo Brown B.

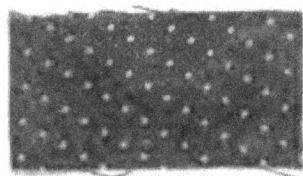

Benzo Green G.

Rose Azurine B.

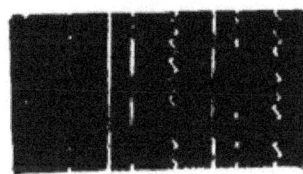

Benzo Sky Blue.

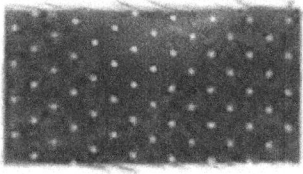

New Toluylene Brown M.

Congo Orange R.

Chrysamine G.

FARBENFABRIKEN vorm. FRIEDR. BAYER & Co., ELBERFELD.

Xyloline Printing.

The Benzidine dyestuffs can also be used for **padding or printing** Xyloline (cotton and paper).

Padding.

No. 1.

1 oz. or 50 grms. **Chloramine Yellow**
12½ galls. „ 100 litres water
2 oz. „ 100 grms. phosphate of soda.

No. 2.

1 oz. or 50 grms. **Geranine G**
12½ galls. „ 100 litres water
2 oz. „ 100 grms. phosphate of soda.

No. 3.

1 oz. or 50 grms. **Heliotrope B B**
12½ galls. „ 100 litres water
2 oz. „ 100 grms. phosphate of soda.

No. 4.

1 oz. or 50 grms. **Brilliant** Benzo Blue 6 B
12½ galls. „ 100 litres water
2 oz. „ 100 grms. phosphate of soda.

Pad on the slop padding machine.

Printing.

No. 5

Orange.

1½ pints or 150 grms. Print colour X
8½ pints „ 850 „ mucilage of tragacanth 65 : 1000
1000 grms.

Print Colour X.

Boil: 8 oz. or 40 grms. **Congo Orange G**
1 lb. „ 50 „ wheat starch and
8½ pints „ 820 „ water, and then add
4 oz. „ 20 „ phosphate of soda
1000 grms.

No. 6.

Blue.

The same as No. 5 but with
8 oz. or 40 grms. **Brilliant Benzo Blue 6 B.**

No. 7.

Violet.

The same as No. 5 but with
8 oz. or 40 grms. **Benzo** Violet R

No. 8.

Brown.

The same as No. 5 but with
8 oz. or 40 grms. **Benzo Chrome Brown B**

No. 9.

Pink.

The same as No. 5 but with
8 oz. or 40 grms. Geranine G.

Steam for ½ hour without pressure.

Xyloline Printing.
(Padded).

Chloramine Yellow.

Geranine G.

Heliotrope B B.

Brilliant Benzo Blue G B.

(Printed).

Congo Orange G.

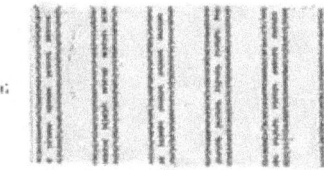

Brilliant Benzo Blue G B.

Benzo Violet R.

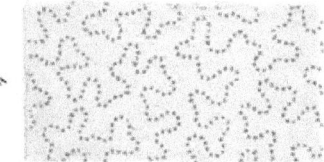

Benzo Chrome Brown B.

Geranine G.

FARBENFABRIKEN vorm. FRIEDR. BAYER & Co., ELBERFELD.

119

Wool Silk Printing.

Many Benzidine Dyestuffs are further well adapted for dyeing mixed goods of wool and silk for dis large purposes.

No. 1.

Dye with 2% Chrysophenine
20% Glauber's salt
and boil for 1 hour.

Steam for ½ hour without pressure, wash and dry.

Discharge with:

6 oz. or 50 grms. Acid Violet **6 B** dissolved in
1½ pints „ 170 „ water, thickened with
5 pints „ 600 „ gum water 1:1, and then add
2½ lbs. „ 200 „ tin crystals
1000 grms.

The following dyestuffs are suitable for colour discharging with tin crystals.
Eosine S extra (yellowish), Quinoline Yellow, Acid Green G G, Fast Acid Blue B etc.

No. 2.

Dye with: 2% **Benzo Chrome Brown R**
20% Glauber's salt.
and boil for 1 hour.

Discharge with:

{ 7½ oz. or 15 grms. **Methylene Blue** B B
{ 1½ „ 85 „ water, thickened with
{ 6¼ pints „ 300 „ gum water 1:1, warm
and then add
10 lbs. „ 320 „ zinc powder, and add
gradually cooling down
with ice,
5 pints „ 280 „ bisulphite of soda 72° Tw.
1000 grms.

Steam for 1 hour without pressure, wash and dry.

No. 3.

Dye with: 2% **Congo Orange R**
20% Glauber's salt.
Boil for 1 hour.

Discharge with:

{ 15 oz. or 30 grms. **Rhoduline Violet** stirred
up with
{ 1½ pints „ 75 „ water, thickened with
{ 6¼ pints „ 300 „ gum water 1:1, warm,
and then add
10 lbs. „ 320 „ zinc powder; finally add
gradually after cooling
with ice
5 pints „ 280 „ bisulphite of soda 72° Tw.

Treatment same as in No. 2.

The following colours can also be similarly employed for dyeing and discharging white: Benzo Chrome Brown G, B, Direct Fast Brown B, Toluylene Brown B, Direct Blue Black N, Diazo Blue Black, Brilliant Geranine B, Geranine G, Delta Purpurine 5B, Benzo Olive, Benzo Sky Blue, Benzo Violet R etc.

Linen Printing.

The Benzidine Dyestuffs are also sometimes used for printing linen.

No. 4.

Boil: 4 oz. or 50 grms. **Chrysophenine**
3½ lbs. „ 300 „ British gum and
6¼ pints „ 650 „ water
1000 grms.

No. 5.

Boil: 8 oz. or 40 grms. **Brilliant Congo R**
3½ lbs. „ 300 „ British gum and
6¼ pints „ 660 „ water
1000 grms.

Print the linen and then steam for 1 hour without pressure.

Wool Silk Printing.
(Discharge Printing.)

Dyed with: 2 Chrysophenine;
discharged with: 3 Acid Violet 6 B.

Dyed with: 2 Benzo Chrome Brown R;
discharged with: 1 Methylene Blue B B.

Dyed with: 2 Benzo Orange R;
discharged with: 3% Rhoduline Violet.

Linen Printing.

Chrysophenine.

Brilliant Congo R.

FARBENFABRIKEN vorm. FRIEDR. BAYER & Co., ELBERFELD.

116

Contents.

Index.

119

Cotton Printing.

For Cotton Printing we further recommend the following approved dyestuffs:
- a. **Basic Dyestuffs** (with tannic acid)
- b. **Mordant Dyestuffs** (with alumina, chrome, iron, nickel, zink)
- c. **Ice Colours.**

Red Dyestuffs:
a.
Brilliant Rhoduline Red B D in paste
Diamond Fuchsine
Pyronine G
Rhodamine B, G, S
Rhoduline Red, B, G
Saffranine F F extra.

b.
Alizarine Red (bluish to yellowish) (alumina)
Alizarine Purpurine in paste (alumina)
Brilliant Chrome Red in paste (chrome)
Chrome Red (chrome)
Eosine (chrome)
Rhodamine, B, G, S (chrome).

c.
Paranitraniline (β-Naphtol or Naphtol L C).

Orange Dyestuffs:
b.
Alizarine Orange (alumina)
Alizarine Yellow R (chrome)
Chrome Orange (chrome)
Diamond Orange (chrome).

Yellow Dyestuffs:
a.
Auramine II.

b.
Alizarine Yellow 3 G (chrome)
Anthracene Yellow in paste (chrome)
Chrome Yellow D (chrome)
Chrome Yellow R extra in paste (chrome)
Diamond Flavine in paste (chrome)
Diamond Yellow in paste (chrome).

Green Dyestuffs:
a.
Brilliant Green
China Green
Emerald Green
Imperial Green
Methyl Green
Turquoise Blue B B, G.

b.
Alizarine Viridine (chrome)
Azo Green in paste (chrome)
Chrome Green (chrome)
Coeruleine S (chrome).

Blue Dyestuffs:
a.
Blue 8336 (Navy Blue)
Cotton Blue I—VI
Methylene Blue B B
New Blue G

New Fast Blue F
New Victoria Blue B
Victoria Blue B.

b.
Alizarine Blue S, S R paste and powder
(chrome, nickel, zinc)
Alizarine Cyanine G, R paste (chrome)
Alkali Blue (chrome)
Brilliant Alizarine Blue G, R, S D, D paste
(chrome)
Celestine Blue B (chrome)
Chrome Blue paste (chrome)
Gallamine Blue (chrome)
Victoria Blue B (chrome).

c.
Dianisidine (β-Naphtol).

Violet Dyestuffs:
a.
Methyl Violet 5 R to 7 B
Rhoduline Violet.

b.
Alizarine Bordeaux B P paste (chrome)
Alizarine Red I, I extra (iron)
Galleine (chrome)
Gallocyanine paste.

Brown and Bordeaux Dyestuffs:
a.
Bismarck Brown F F, F, R extra, R, M.

b.
Alizarine Bordeaux B P, G P paste (alumina)
Alizarine Cardinal paste (alumina)
Alizarine Orange (chrome)
Alizarine Purpurine paste (chrome)
Alizarine Red (yellow — blue shade) (chrome)
Anthracene Brown G G, G, R, W paste (chrome)
Chrome Brown R paste (chrome)
Chrome Bordeaux (Chrome)
Chrome Bordeaux 6 B double (chrome)
Chrome Prune (chrome)
Chrome Rubine (chrome)
Diamond Brown G (chrome).

c.
Alpha Naphtylamine (β-Naphtol)
Benzidine (β-Naphtol)
Mononitro Benzidine (β-Naphtol).

Grey Dyestuffs:
a.
New Fast Grey
New Grey P paste.

b.
Alizarine Blue Black B paste (chrome)
Alizarine Cyanine Black G paste (chrome)
Alizarine Fast Grey paste (chrome).

Black Dyestuffs:
a.
Jute Black.

b.
Alizarine Blue Black B paste (chrome)
Alizarine Bordeaux B P paste (chrome)
Alizarine Cyanine Black G paste (chrome)
Alizarine Fast Grey paste (chrome)
Chrome Black (chrome).

c.
Benzidine (Developer E S).

Wool and Half Wool Printing.

For printing wool and half wool we recommend the following approved dyestuffs:

a. Acid Dyestuffs
b. Mordant Dyestuffs (chrome or alumina)
c. Basic Dyestuffs.

Red Dyestuffs:
a.
Acid Magenta
Azo Bordeaux
Azo Crimson S
Azo Eosine
Azo Fuchsine B, C, G extra
Bordeaux B X, extra
Brilliant Double Scarlet 3 R
Brilliant Ponceau 5 R
Carmoisine B
Cochineal Scarlet P S
Croceine Scarlet 2 B, 3 B X, 7 B, 10 B
Double Ponceau 4 R
Eosine S extra bluish (for pink)
Fast Acid Magenta B
Fast Red A, B T, E, N S
New Coccine
Orseilline B B
Ponceau 3 R
Rhodamine B, G (for pink)
Wool Ponceau 2 R
b.
Alizarine Purpurine paste (alumina)
Alizarine Red II A B 20 % (alumina)
Alizarine Red W powder (alumina)
Anthracene Red (chrome)
Cloth Red B (chrome)
c.
Rhoduline Red B, G
Safranine F F extra.

Orange Dyestuffs:
a.
Croceine Orange G, R
Eosine S extra yellowish
Orange II B.
b.
Alizarine Orange (alumina).

Yellow Dyestuffs:
a.
Fast Yellow extra
Indian Yellow G, R
Metanil Yellow
Naphtol Yellow S
Quinoline Yellow.
b.
Alizarine Yellow 3 G (chrome)
Anthracene Yellow (chrome)
Chrome Yellow D, R extra (chrome)
Diamond Flavine G (chrome).
c.
Auramine II.

Green Dyestuffs:
a.
Acid Green B B, 3 B, G G
Alizarine Cyanine Green K, G extra paste
Fast Green bluish, yellowish
Fast Green extra bluish
Fast Light Green
b.
Alizarine Cyanine Green G extra, E paste
Chrome Green (chrome)   [(chrome)
Coeruleine (chrome).
c.
Brilliant Green
Turquoise Blue G.

Blue Dyestuffs:
a.
Alizarine Sapphirole
Alkali Blue 1 B—7 B
Azine Blue
Brilliant Alizarine Cyanine G, 3 G
Carmine Blue B. G
Fast Acid Blue B
Fast Acid Violet 10 B
Fast Blue greenish
IndulME B, 6 B greenish
Navy Blue
New Patent Blue 4 B.
b.
Alizarine Blue S, S R paste and powder
Alizarine Cyanine (chrome)   [(chrome)
Alizarine Sapphirole (chrome)
Brilliant Alizarine Blue G, R (chrome)
Brilliant Alizarine Cyanine G, 3 G (chrome)
Chrome Blue (chrome)
Gallamine Blue (chrome).
c.
Blue 8336 (Navy Blue)
New Victoria Blue B
Victoria Blue B

Violet Dyestuffs:
a.
Acid Violet 3 B extra, 4 B G extra, 4 B extra,
       5 B, 6 B, 8 B extra, 4 R S, 6 B N,
       1 R extra, 2 R, 3 R.
Alkali Violet R
Azo Acid Violet B extra, R extra
Azo Acid Violet 4 R
Victoria Violet 5 B.
b.
Celestine Blue B (chrome)
Gallcine (chrome).
c.
Methyl Violet 5 R 7 B.

Brown Dyestuffs:
a.
Azo Acid Brown.
b.
Alizarine Cardinal (chrome)
Alizarine Orange (chrome)
Alizarine Red II A B 20 % (chrome)
Alizarine Red W powder (chrome)
Anthracene Brown (chrome)
Chrome Brown (chrome).
c.
Bismarck Brown.

Grey Dyestuffs:
a.
Nigrosine B.
c.
New Fast Grey
New Grey P paste.

Black Dyestuffs:
a.
Diamond Black F
Victoria Black B, G.
b.
Alizarine Cyanine Black G (chrome)
Alizarine Blue Black B (chrome).
Alizarine Fast Grey (chrome).
c.
Jute Black B.

Silk and Half Silk Printing.

For printing silk and half silk we recommend the following approved dyestuffs:
- **a. Basic Dyestuffs** (with tannic acid)
- **b. Mordant Dyestuffs** (with chrome or alumina)
- **c. Acid Dyestuffs.**

Red Dyestuffs:

a.
Brilliant Rhoduline Red B D paste
Diamond Fuchsine
Rhodamine B, G
Rhoduline Red B G
Saffranine F F extra.

b.
Alizarine Red S X extra (alumina)
Alizarine Red W powder (alumina)
Alizarine Red I P (alumina)
Brilliant Chrome Red (chrome)
Chrome Red (chrome).

c.
Anthracene Red
Azo Bordeaux
Azo Fuchsine G
Azo Crimson S
Brilliant Croceine
Brilliant Double Scarlet 3 R
Brilliant Ponceau 5 R
Carmoisine B
Cochineal Scarlet P S
Croceine Scarlet 3 B X, 2 B X
Double Ponceau 4 R
Fast Red X S
Fast Acid Magenta B
Imperial Scarlet 3 B
New Coccine.

Orange Dyestuffs:

b.
Alizarine Orange (alumina)
Chrome Orange (chrome).

c.
Orange II B.

Yellow Dyestuffs:

a.
Auramine II.

b.
Anthracene Yellow (chrome)
Chrome Yellow D (chrome)
Chrome Yellow R extra (chrome)
Diamond Flavine G (chrome)
Diamond Yellow (chrome).

Green Dyestuffs:

a.
Brilliant Green
China Green
Emerald Green
Imperial Green
Methyl Green
Turquoise Blue B B, G.

b.
Alizarine Cyanine Green G extra (chrome)
Chrome Green (chrome)
Coeruleine (chrome).

c.
Acid Green G G
Fast Green bluish
Fast Green extra bluish
New Patent Blue B.

Blue Dyestuffs:

a.
Blue 8336 (Navy Blue)
Methylene Blue B B
New Blue
New Fast Blue F.

b.
Alizarine Blue S, S R paste and powder
Alizarine Cyanine G G (chrome) (chrome)
Brilliant Alizarine Blue G, S D (chrome)
Chrome Blue paste (chrome).

c.
Azo Acid Blue 4 B
Fast Acid Blue B
Fast Acid Violet 10 B
Induline B, 6 B
Intensive Blue
New Patent Blue 4 B
Silk Blue B E S
Soluble Blue red shade extra strong
Sulphon Acid Blue B, R.

Violet Dyestuffs:

a.
Methyl Violet 5 R — 7 B
Rhoduline Violet.

b.
Alizarine Bordeaux B P paste (chrome)
Alizarine Cyanine R paste (alumina)
Chrome Violet paste (chrome)
Galleine paste (chrome).

c.
Acid Violet 5 B, R extra, 2 R, 3 R
Azo Acid Violet R extra
Victoria Violet 5 B.

Brown and Bordeaux Dyestuffs:

a
Bismarck Brown F, F F, R extra, R, M.

b.
Alizarine Bordeaux paste (alumina)
Alizarine Orange (chrome)
Alizarine Red R A B (chrome)
Alizarine Red W powder (chrome)
Anthracene Brown (chrome)
Chrome Bordeaux (chrome)
Diamond Brown G (chrome).

Grey Dyestuffs:

a.
New Fast Grey
New Grey paste.

Black Dyestuffs:

a.
Jute Black.

b
Alizarine Cyanine Black G (chrome).

www.ingramcontent.com/pod-product-compliance
Lightning Source LLC
Chambersburg PA
CBHW030619270326
41927CB00007B/1238